I0199914

Caspar Barlaeus

The Wise Merchant

Caspar Barlaeus

The Wise Merchant

Edited by Anna-Luna Post
Critical text and translation by Corinna Vermeulen

Routledge
Taylor & Francis Group
LONDON AND NEW YORK

First published in 2019 by Amsterdam University Press Ltd.

Published 2025 by Routledge
4 Park Square, Milton Park, Abingdon, Oxon OX14 4RN
605 Third Avenue, New York, NY 10158

Routledge is an imprint of the Taylor & Francis Group, an informa business

© All authors / Taylor & Francis Group 2019

The Open Access version of this book, available at www.taylorfrancis.com, has been made available under a Creative Commons Attribution-NonCommercial-NoDerivatives (CC-BY- NC-ND) 4.0 International license.

Trademark notice: Product or corporate names may be trademarks or registered trademarks, and are used only for identification and explanation without intent to infringe.

ISBN: 9789462988002 (hbk)
ISBN: 9781041189381 (pbk)
ISBN: 9781003708117 (ebk)
NUR 685

Cover illustration: Maria van Oosterwijck, *Vanitas Still Life* (1668), KHM-Museumsverband

Cover design: Coördesign, Leiden

DOI: 10.5117/9789462988002

For Product Safety Concerns and Information please contact our EU representative: GPSR@taylorandfrancis.com
Taylor & Francis Verlag GmbH, Kaufingerstraße 24, 80331 München, Germany

Contents

Acknowledgements

This publication of Caspar Barlaeus' celebrated oration would not have been possible without generous funding from three different organizations and the help of several individuals.

We would like to thank Utrecht University for funding the translation of the text into English – a good example of this institution's continued dedication to the internationalization of higher education. The Vossius Center for the History of the Humanities and Sciences and the Thijssen-Schoute Foundation have both contributed generously to this publication.

The researchers of Utrecht University's Department of Early Modern Dutch Literature discussed an early version of the introduction, and Frans Blom, Dirk van Miert and Arthur Weststeijn commented on later versions. Anna-Luna Post is grateful for their helpful insights and kind words, and for Christien Franken's help in improving the English.

We have each written our share of the notes to the translation. We are greatly indebted to Sape van der Woude's extensive notes to his edition and translation of Barlaeus' oration. The same applies to Catherine Secretan's French translation. Corinna Vermeulen would like to thank Marlein van Raalte for identifying several Greek quotations.

Anna-Luna Post & Corinna Vermeulen

Introduction: wealth, knowledge and prestige

On 9 January 1632, Amsterdam was a prospering city. In some 50 years, its population had more than tripled to over 100,000 inhabitants, and the city continued to expand rapidly. The newly constructed canal girdle offered space to its increasingly self-assured elite, and the new houses functioned both as living spaces, home offices and storage units. Their inhabitants not only belonged to the city's economic elite, but also formed its political core, fulfilling posts in the city militia and urban government. Conveniently, the *Wisselbank* (Bank of Amsterdam), Bourse and city hall were within walking distance of their homes, as were the numerous printing houses and bookshops on the Rokin and Kalverstraat. These offered a welcome diversion and intellectual stimulation to the hard-working, always busy merchants.[1]

The source of all this growing wealth and prosperity was trade: by this time, Amsterdam had become one of the most important trading cities in Europe. The Dutch East India Company (VOC) had been in business for 30 years, and many canal houses stocked large supplies of sugar, spices and other exotic goods. Profits were used to further invest in trade, but also in city planning and real estate. The construction of new neighbourhoods and the reclaiming of land outside the city provided profit and prestige to investors, but also quickly led to corruption and scandals, as the city's political elite used these projects for flagrant self-enrichment. Nonetheless, Amsterdam explicitly and proudly celebrated its commercial identity, for instance in the poem Jan Vos wrote for the new Bourse. In this poem, which was printed on several maps and medals, Vos

---

1   C. Lesger, 'Merchants in Charge: The Self-Perception of Amsterdam Merchants, ca. 1550-1700', in M.C. Jacob and C. Secretan (eds.), *The Self-Perception of Early Modern Capitalists* (New York 2008) 75-97, 75, 79-82.

equates Amsterdam's Bourse with several ancient examples of greatness:

> Ephesus' fame was her temple
> Tyre her market and her port
> Babylon her masonry Walls
> Memphis her pyramids
> Rome her empire
> All the world praises me.[2]

The commercial hustle and bustle of Amsterdam was not to everyone's liking. In a letter to his friend and fellow scholar Arnold Buchelius, the famous humanist and poet Caspar Barlaeus compared the quietude of Leiden to the crowded chaos of Amsterdam, and also said he would rather live in Utrecht than 'between these merchants and gainful men.'[3] Barlaeus had been trained as a minister and doctor but provided for his family by writing and offering private tuition. He consequently associated

---

2   The original reads 'Roemt Ephesus op haer kerk / Tyrhus op haer markt en haven / Babel op haer metzelwerk / Memphis op haer spitze gaven/ Romein op haer heerschappy / Al de werelt roemt op my', in E.A. Sutton, *Capitalism and Cartography in the Dutch Golden Age* (Chicago 2015) 55 (transl. Sutton). Also see ibidem, 55-67, on the Beemster, and C. Lesger, *Handel in Amsterdam ten tijde van de Opstand. Kooplieden, commerciële expansie en verandering in de ruimtelijke economie van de Nederlanden ca. 1550-ca.1630* (Hilversum 2001) 171-172 on corrupt politicians.

3   Caspar Barlaeus to Arnoud Buchelius (Aernout van Buchel), 16 April 1631: 'Ad Calendas Maji hinc abitum paro, Amstelodamum migraturus, ex quieta in turbulentam & negotiosam urbem. Nihil est quod eo me rapiat, praeterquam melioris famae solatium, alioqui plura sunt, quae me hic detinere possint, eruditorum frequentia, Academica studia, loci amoenitas, assuetudo, aliaque. Si Ultrajectinis illud fuisset institutum, quod jam est Amstelodamensibus, maluissem in vestra urbe vivere, quam inter Mercuriales & quaestuosos homines.' Letter 175 in *Briefwisseling van Caspar Barlaeus (1584-1648)*, after the edition of Geeraerd Brandt (Amsterdam 1667), edited by M. van Zuylen and A.J.E. Harmsen, available on www.let.leidenuniv.nl/ Dutch/Latijn/BarlaeusEpistolae.html, accessed 22 February 2018. All translations are by the author, unless otherwise stated. Translations of Barlaeus' oration are of course by Corinna Vermeulen.

Amsterdam with the low pursuit of trade, rather than with his own most coveted enterprise: learning. This association was, perhaps, not surprising: the one thing Amsterdam's elite inhabitants could not reach by foot was a university. In 1575 Leiden was chosen as the preferred spot for a university in the newly founded Dutch Republic. Its unique privilege in the province of Holland effectively prevented Amsterdam from establishing its own university. As Amsterdam grew, this lack of a prestigious institution became more conspicuous; it was not only inconvenient, but also contributed to the negative perception of its inhabitants as men who only valued money.

Barlaeus was not the only one to condemn Amsterdam's inhabitants for their mercantile spirit and lack of learning. Although trade brought numerous advantages to the city as well as to the Republic at large, Amsterdam was still frequently looked down upon and disapproved of. Ancient as well as Christian thought viewed merchants as unreliable crooks and trade as an unsuitable occupation for men of honour, as it required its practitioners to lie, manipulate and deceive.[4] And yet, within a year of his disdainful remarks on Amsterdam's merchants, Barlaeus publicly spoke in defence of trade and its practitioners. On 9 January 1632, he delivered a long and compelling oration on the fruitful combination of trade and philosophy: *Mercator sapiens, sive oratio de conjungendis mercaturae et philosophiae studiis*, or *The Wise Merchant: Oration on Combining the Pursuits of Trade and Philosophy*.

He spoke on the occasion of the opening of the Athenaeum Illustre, Amsterdam's Illustrious school: the closest thing to a university the city was able to establish without interfering with Leiden's privilege.[5] The aim of the Illustrious School was

4   See C. Lis and H. Soly, *Worthy Efforts: Attitudes to Work and Workers in Pre-Industrial Europe* (Leiden and Boston 2012) 263-273, for the discussion on trade in the sixteenth- and seventeenth-century Republic.
5   D. van Miert, *Humanism in an Age of Science, The Amsterdam Athenaeum in the Golden Age, 1632-1704* (Leiden and Boston 2009) 21-34; M. Prak, *The Dutch Republic in the Seventeenth Century: The Golden Age* (Cambridge 2005) 30.

to provide education for the sons of the city's elite: boys who had finished their early education at one of the Latin schools, but were still deemed too young to attend university in a foreign town, or lacked the necessary philosophical background. The lectures, provided by two professors – one in history, one in philosophy – were to take place each morning and would be open to the broader public, thus enabling the young boys' fathers to attend as well. After some delay, the Athenaeum Illustre opened its doors on 8 January 1632, with the inaugural address of its new history professor, Gerardus Johannes Vossius.

Barlaeus spoke the day after Vossius and made the combination of philosophy and trade the explicit subject of his oration. He argued throughout that the relation between them was not necessarily one of tension, but rather one of mutual benefit, and he cited numerous ancient authors to support his case. This theme made the oration uniquely suited to capture the interest of his audience and of many later readers. The oration was swiftly published by Willem Jansz. Blaeu, and two Dutch translations appeared within 30 years of its first deliverance.[6] The original Latin text also opened the collection of Barlaeus' orations, which first came out in 1643 and appeared in two later editions as well.[7] The oration thus quickly gained recognition in humanist circles in Amsterdam and the Dutch Republic at large. Barlaeus' text has stood the test of time: his oration has continued to draw the attention of Dutch scholars and publicists throughout the 20th and 21st centuries. In 1969, Sape van der Woude issued a Dutch translation accompanied by a brief introduction, which has

---

6   D. van Netten, *Koopman in Kennis: De uitgever Willem Jansz Blaeu in de geleerde wereld (1571–1638)* (Zutphen 2014) 175. The first Dutch translation by Wilhelmus Buyserius appeared in 1641 in Enkhuyzen, the second (by Jan van Duisburgh) was published in the Dutch edition of Barlaeus' collected speeches in 1662. See C. Secretan (ed.), *Le 'Marchand philosophe' de Caspar Barlaeus. Un éloge du commerce dans la Hollande du Siècle d'Or. Étude, texte et traduction du Mercator Sapiens* (Paris 2002) 100-101.

7   A. Weststeijn, *Commercial Republicanism in the Dutch Golden Age: The Political Thought of Johan and Pieter de la Court* (Leiden and Boston 2012) 188, n176.

inspired countless scholars to include the term 'mercator sapiens' in their articles about merchants, agents or publishers with an interest in science or the scholarly life.[8] The prominent public historian Geert Mak has even called for a revival of the *mercator sapiens*, arguing that the modern Netherlands lacks a proper elite that truly fulfils an exemplary function and combines the pursuit of wealth with that of wisdom, as it did in seventeenth-century Amsterdam.[9]

More recently, the oration has also sparked the interest of an international readership. The seemingly straightforward oration has been portrayed as an archetypical text that uniquely captures the spirit of the Dutch Golden Age, by celebrating the merging of trade and wisdom. Harold Cook argues that the text shows 'that the values inherent in the world of commerce were explicitly and self-consciously recognized to be at the root of the new science by contemporaries'.[10] Cook's interpretation of Barlaeus' oration has drawn criticism, however, especially by scholars who firmly place Barlaeus' text in the context of Renaissance humanism.[11] Most recently, Catherine Secretan, the oration's French translator, has argued that the text offers a legitimation of merchants' active participation on the world stage, through the lessons of the ancients and recent authors in the tradition of Erasmian

8   M. Peters, *De wijze koopman: Het wereldwijde onderzoek van Nicolaes Witsen (1641-1717), burgemeester en VOC-bewindhebber van Amsterdam* (Amsterdam 2010) and M. Keblusek, 'Mercator Sapiens: Merchants as Cultural Entrepreneurs', in B. Noldus and M. Keblusek (eds.), *Double Agents: Cultural and Political Brokerage in Early Modern Europe* (Leiden and Boston 2009), are just two recent examples; many more can be found, as van Netten, *Koopman in Kennis* 175, has also pointed out.

9   G. Mak, 'De kooplieden van Amsterdam: Leve Spinoza, leve Gümüs, leve de mercator sapiens!' in *De Groene Amsterdammer* (30 november 2002); G. Mak, 'Wij, de elites van nu, missen noblesse oblige' and 'Wij, de elite van deze tijd, zijn veel te bang' in *NRC Handelsblad* (18 April 2015).

10   H. Cook, *Matters of Exchange: Commerce, Medicine and Science in the Dutch Golden Age* (New Haven 2007) 68.

11   K. van Berkel, 'Rediscovering Clusius. How Dutch Commerce Contributed to the Emergence of Modern Science', *BMGN – Low Countries Historical Review*, vol. 123, no. 2 (2008) 233; Van Miert, *Humanism in an Age of Science* 226-228; Weststeijn, *Commercial Republicanism* 184-190.

humanism.[12] The authors of *Worthy Efforts: Attitudes to Work and Workers in Pre-Industrial Europe*, who consider the speech to be 'one long ode to businessmen, without any reservations', have followed this interpretation.[13]

Yet, Barlaeus' oration is much more complex than appears at first sight. Rather than an unequivocal appraisal of the pursuits of trade and wisdom on equal grounds, Barlaeus firmly argues that wisdom ought to be valued over trade. Similarly, while Barlaeus seemingly offered a straightforward endorsement of the activities of merchants and traders, he also issued covert and less covert warnings to them and to the city's government. In addition, Barlaeus used his opening address to strike a chord with the merchants of Amsterdam and to win them for his cause: the study of ancient texts. He clearly explained this purpose in a letter to his close friend Constantijn Huygens, sent several days after he delivered his inaugural address: 'It is our intention that the merchants take to the taste of it [i.e. the lectures] and that we arouse in them a love for these studies, from which they have until now held themselves at some considerable distance.'[14]

Thus, rather than as an endorsement of trade, the oration as a whole should be read as a long and detailed *captatio benevolentiae* – a rhetorical strategy to induce the audience's goodwill for the Athenaeum Illustre. Barlaeus' stress on knowledge and wisdom as keys to better trade, government, and, more generally, life itself, rendered the Athenaeum Illustre an attractive undertaking to Amsterdam's elite. At the same time, Barlaeus also found a way to criticize the society developing in the Dutch Golden Age: he presented the example of the virtuous, wise merchant as one that should be followed by his public and their offspring, and warned those who would not heed his advice. This double-sided reasoning is at the core of Barlaeus' oration.

12 Secretan, *Le 'Marchand philosophe'* 13.
13 Lis and Soly, *Worthy Efforts* 264.
14 F.F. Blok, *From the Correspondence of a Melancholic* (Assen 1976) 17 (transl. Blok).

Portrait of Caspar Barlaeus in 1625, by Willem Jacobsz Delff. Rijksmuseum, Amsterdam

Barlaeus himself phrased it best: 'I have chosen a subject that in my opinion suited the character of this city and its citizens as well as the interests of a very wealthy trade centre – imitating fishermen who attach a decoy to the hook, an enticing bait.'[15] The metaphor is strikingly appropriate. Barlaeus chose an attractive, seductive subject to draw in Amsterdam's administrators, merchants and youth; yet, that enticing bait hides a much more serious message that suits his interests rather than theirs. Like Barlaeus' audience, historians have frequently been reeled in by this bait, while overlooking the hook and its fisherman. What we need to do, instead, is to analyse the text as a whole and in more detail, asking what Barlaeus aimed to achieve with this text, and how the main argument is related to that aim. In doing so, we are able to highlight how the humanist scholar tried to please his audience while simultaneously warning it against the risks of the commercialization of society. We may then further probe the significance of the text, and question some of its earlier interpretations. This can only be achieved by placing the oration – and its author – in its particular context. Thus, this introduction discusses the founding of the Athenaeum Illustre, Barlaeus' life, career and relation with his colleague Gerardus Johannes Vossius, as well as the influence of ancient philosophy and Renaissance humanism on the *Mercator sapiens*.

Barlaeus' life and career

In his funerary oration, delivered on 16 January 1648, the jurist Johannes Arnoldus Corvinus (born Joannes Arnoldsz Raevens) listed the many achievements of his late colleague at the Athenaeum Illustre. Among them was a surprising number of publications, both poetry and prose, on an astonishing range of subjects. It is quite an accomplishment that Barlaeus managed to combine this wealth of publications with his many other

---

15   Barlaeus, *The Wise Merchant* 77, 3-6.

endeavours – for Barlaeus' career was really quite remarkable. He had started out as minister in the small town of Nieuw Tongen in 1609, and had subsequently become sub-regent of the *Collegium Theologicum* (The States' College or Statencollege in Leiden, financed by the States of Holland, which prepared young men for a career as minister). In 1619, he took up the study of medicine at Caen and completed his degree in just two years. Yet, rather than practise his new profession, during the 1620s Barlaeus made a living by tutoring students and offering them room and board. For several years, he supplemented the income from these activities with his poetic endeavours, occasionally lamenting his dependence on others. Yet, Corvinus' funerary oration presented Barlaeus as 'Doctor of Medicine, and Professor of all of Philosophy for the Illustrious School of Amsterdam'.[16] How, – and why –, one might ask, did Barlaeus go from minister, to doctor, poet, private tutor, and finally, to professor of philosophy?

Caspar van Baerle was born in Antwerp on 12 February 1584. Like many Protestants from the Southern Netherlands, Barlaeus' parents moved to Leiden in 1586 after the fall of Antwerp. Two years later Caspar's father was appointed rector of the Latin school in Zaltbommel, a town located near the Waal river. His uncle Jacob occupied the same post in Den Briel (near the coast). When the young Caspar lost his father in 1595, this uncle took over the task of raising him. The boy showed a talent for learning and, at the age of sixteen, Caspar Barlaeus started as a theology student at the States' College. He completed his propaedeutic programme in Latin, Greek, Hebrew and philosophy within three

---

16   In the title of Boëthius Van Elslandt's Dutch translation of Corvinus' speech: *Lyk-Reden op 't overlyden van den wydt-beroemden Caspar van Baerle, Doctor in de Medecijnen en Professor van de gantsche Philosophie in de doorluchtige Schole tot Amsterdam, uitgesproken door Johannes Arnoldus Corvinus* (Amsterdam 1648). Van Elslandt was a student of Barlaeus; see K. Bostoen, 'De Van Elstlands: Een Haarlems Poëtengeslacht' in E.K. Grootes (ed.), *Haarlems Helicon: Literatuur en Toneel te Haarlem vóór 1800* (Hilversum 1993) 123-138, 123.

years, followed by another three years of study – now in theology proper.[17]

Shortly after completing his education, Barlaeus received his first appointment as minister in Nieuw Tongen. Only two years later he was named sub-regent of the States' College and, thus, returned to his alma mater to teach there and assist the regent of the college. When in 1615 a new regent was appointed, Barlaeus was joined by Gerardus Vossius.[18] Vossius was Barlaeus' senior by seven years, and had also attended the States' College. The similarities did not end there: about fifteen years later, both men would be asked to become the first professors at the newly founded Athenaeum Illustre. Before that, however, they both lost their positions at the States' College due to their religious stances.[19]

In the second decade of the seventeenth century, the young Republic was ridden by a new religious conflict that had profound influences on the new state and its inhabitants. Against the background of the Twelve Years' Truce, internal struggles came to the fore, and one of these entailed the proper interpretation of the Calvinist doctrine of predestination. The conflict arose in 1604 and initially its two main players were Franciscus Gomarus, professor of theology at the University of Leiden, and his colleague Jacobus Arminius. Arminius, leader of the Remonstrant party, employed a more lenient interpretation

17   S. Van der Woude (ed.), *Mercator Sapiens. Oratie gehouden bij de inwijding van de illustere school te Amsterdam op 9 januari 1632*. Dutch translation and introduction by S. van der Woude (Amsterdam 1967) 8-9. See also J.A. Worp, 'Caspar van Baerle I. Zijne jeugd, studententijd en predikambt (1584-1612)', *Oud-Holland*, vol. 3 (1885) 241-265.

18   F.F. Blok, 'Caspar Barlaeus, de filosoof van het Athenaeum Illustre', in C.L. Heesakkers, C.S.M. Rademaker and F.F. Blok, *Vossius en Barlaeus: Twee helden die der dingen diept en steilt'afpeilen. Het Athenaeum Illustre en zijn eerste hoogleraren* (Amsterdam 1982) 24.

19   Van der Woude, *Mercator Sapiens* 11. For more on Barlaeus' years at the Statencollege and his efforts to advance the Remonstrant cause, see J.A. Worp, 'Caspar van Baerle II: Barlaeus als onder-regent van het Statencollege (1612-1619)', *Oud-Holland*, vol. 4 (1886) 24-40.

of the doctrine of predestination, while Gomarus, head of the Counter-Remonstrants, argued for a stricter interpretation.[20] Both Barlaeus and Vossius sided with the Arminians in this conflict; a choice that would greatly influence their lives and careers. This was especially true for Barlaeus, who had signed the Five Articles of Remonstrance (*Remonstrantie*) in 1610. In the years to come, he would actively participate in heated debates on the subject, and in 1618 he even attended the national Synod of Dort, where delegates representing both groups tried to settle the controversy.[21] In the meantime, the conflict had spiralled into the political realm, leading to the arrest of grand pensionary (*raadpensionaris*) Johan van Oldenbarnevelt by the stadholder, prince Maurice of Orange. At the final meeting of the Synod, which took place on 9 May 1619, the conflict was decided in favour of the Counter-Remonstrants. As a result, the Remonstrants were excluded from important positions, and consequently Barlaeus, at this time professor in Logic at Leiden University, was fired from his post.[22]

Barlaeus knew his Remonstrant sympathies would be an obstacle to a renewed career as a theologian, and therefore aimed to take up a new and potentially lucrative profession: medicine. He must have hoped this career shift would enable him to provide for his family: in 1608, he married Barbara Sayon, and by 1619 they already had four children. The former theologian swiftly received his medicine degree, and equally quickly discovered that the new occupation did not suit him well. Barlaeus had a sensitive constitution and found it difficult to be confronted with human fragility. He, therefore, never pursued his new profession,

20   J. Israel, *The Dutch Republic: Its Rise, Greatness and Fall, 1477-1806* (Oxford 1995) chapters 18-20 give an extensive account of the conflict and its broader implications. See Prak, *The Dutch Republic* 29-37, for a succinct overview of the main developments.

21   Van der Woude, *Mercator Sapiens* 9.

22   Blok, *From The Correspondence of A Melancholic* 2. For more on this conflict and the influence it had on Barlaeus see Worp, 'Caspar van Baerle III. Zijn verder verblijf te Leiden (1619-1631)', *Oud-Holland*, vol. 4 (1886) 172-189.

and instead provided for his family by offering private tuition, room and board to students.[23]

Barlaeus supplemented this modest income by writing laudatory and marriage poetry on commission, and evidently had more success as a poet than as a doctor. He became a very prolific writer and even earned the epithet 'Prince of the Poets', assigned to him by his friend Hugo Grotius.[24] Barlaeus' network of influential scholars was a useful asset: the friendship he struck up with Constantijn Huygens in 1625 would prove particularly fruitful. Huygens introduced Barlaeus to other potential national and international patrons, and functioned as a broker by circulating his works at court. Most importantly, Huygens recommended the poetic skills of his new acquaintance to stadholder Frederick Henry, who would become Barlaeus' most important patron.[25] From 1625 onward, Barlaeus regularly celebrated Frederick Henry's military pursuits and special family occasions in verse.[26] His efforts were rewarded with occasional gifts from the stadholder, and from 1635 onward, Barlaeus even received regular monetary support from the stadholder in the form of a pension.[27]

During this period, Barlaeus' reputation sufficiently prospered to be considered an ideal candidate when the burgomasters of Amsterdam started their search for a professor to lead the Athenaeum Illustre. Barlaeus, however, did not wholeheartedly welcome their invitation. He complained of his dependence on

23 Van der Woude, *Mercator Sapiens* 11-12, and Worp, 'Caspar van Baerle III. Zijn verder verblijf te Leiden' 176-177.
24 Secretan, *Le 'Marchand philosophe'* 31.
25 Worp, 'Caspar van Baerle III. Zijn verder verblijf te Leiden' 179-181.
26 Between 1625 and 1647, Barlaeus wrote seven works celebrating Frederick Henry's military pursuits and two works concerning the stadholder's children Willem and Louise. He also composed a funeral oration for the stadholder in 1647. Barlaeus further wrote two works praising Johan Maurits van Nassau. In L.D. Petit, *Bibliographische lijst der werken van de Leidsche hoogleeraren van de oprichting der hoogeschool tot op onze dagen*, vol. I (Leiden 1894) 193-221.
27 Blok, *From The Correspondence of A Melancholic* 5; Worp, 'Caspar van Baerle III. Zijn verder verblijf te Leiden' 180; Worp, 'Caspar van Baerle IV. Eerste jaren te Amsterdam (1631-1635)', *Oud-Holland*, vol. 5 (1887) 98, 101.

others, writing Huygens: 'I am like a piece of land, which, as it does not have an owner, falls to the first person who sits down on it.'[28] This was a complaint he had voiced before, both in letters and in poems, and one that was uttered more often by writers who depended on their literary output for their income. Barlaeus was also reluctant to leave Leiden for Amsterdam, which he did not care for much – as we have already seen.[29] Still, Barlaeus appreciated the opportunity offered to him and, regardless of his complaints, accepted. He particularly looked forward to the freedom the city would offer him: in Amsterdam, he would be able to speak his mind more freely while simultaneously enjoying the advantages and stability of a fixed position.[30]

Although Barlaeus would finally enjoy a stable salary (of no less than 1,500 guilders) at the Athenaeum, he did not give up his writing. On the contrary, he proved especially productive in the period 1632–1648.[31] The move to Amsterdam allowed him to expand his network, resulting in several poems celebrating the

28 Van der Woude, *Mercator Sapiens* 13: 'Ik ben gelijk een stuk land dat, daar het geen eigenaar heeft, toekomt aan de eerste de beste die er zich op neer zet.' Original Latin in Worp, 'Caspar van Baerle III. Zijn verder verblijf in Leiden (1619-1631). Vervolg' 248, n9.

29 From Barlaeus' correspondence, letter 175 to Buchelius, 16 April 1631: 'Ad Calendas Maji hinc abitum paro, Amstelodamum migraturus, ex quieta in turbulentam & negotiosam urbem. Nihil est quod eo me rapiat, praeterquam melioris famae solatium, alioqui plura sunt, quae me hic detinere possint, eruditorum frequentia, Academica studia, loci amoenitas, assuetudo, aliaque. Si Ultrajectinis illud fuisset institutum, quod jam est Amstelodamensibus, maluissem in vestra urbe vivere, quam inter Mercuriales & quaestuosos homines.' See also C.L. Heesakkers, 'Het Athenaeum Illustre', in C.L. Heesakkers, C.S.M. Rademaker and F.F. Blok (eds.), *Vossius en Barlaeus: Twee helden die der dingen diept en steilt'afpeilen. Het Athenaeum Illustre en zijn eerste hoogleraren* (Amsterdam 1982) 5; and Van der Woude, *Mercator Sapiens* 13.

30 See Blok, *From the Correspondence of a Melancholic*, 10-11; Worp, 'Caspar van Baerle III. Zijn verder verblijf te Leiden (1619-1631). Vervolg' 251, on the freer atmosphere in Amsterdam.

31 See Petit, *Bibliographische lijst* 193-221; A.J.E. Harmsen and E. Hofland, *Bibliografie van Caspar Barlaeus*, category C: Not in Petit. Via www.let.leidenuniv.nl/Dutch/Latijn/BarlaeusBibliografie.html, accessed 22 February 2018.

marriages of Amsterdam regents or their family members. The poem written for Eva Bicker's marriage to Dirck de Graeff in 1629 seems to suggest that Barlaeus already sought to become embedded in the Amsterdam network before his official appointment to the Athenaeum.[32] Not only was Eva Bicker the direct cousin of Andries Bicker, one of the four burgomasters who had invited Barlaeus to Amsterdam, but Dirck's father Jacob Dircksz. de Graeff would serve as one of the curators of the Athenaeum in 1632. Dirck de Graeff had been a student of Barlaeus in Leiden, and the two men kept in touch after De Graeff had finished his studies.[33] The poem Barlaeus wrote in his honour might perhaps be a clue as to why Amsterdam's regents immediately approached Barlaeus when they sought a professor for the Athenaeum.

The families Bicker and De Graeff formed a strong alliance in Amsterdam, and ensured a more lenient climate for the Remonstrants in the city.[34] Seen in this light, Barlaeus' poem celebrating the marriage of their offspring in 1629 gains further significance. In the years to follow, Barlaeus ensured the consolidation of his new-found connection with these powerful families. In 1633, Barlaeus wrote a poem to celebrate the marriage of Cornelis de Graeff – Dirck's brother –, to Geertrui Overlander. When Eva Bicker remarried after the death of her first husband Dirck, Barlaeus also provided a poem to praise her marriage to Frederik Alewijn.[35] Barlaeus further dedicated his poem in celebration of Maria de Medici's official visit to

32 Petit, *Bigliographische Lijst,* entry 33. The poem was published in Leiden in 1630, and reprinted – in collected works – several times over the course of the seventeenth century.
33 Worp, 'Caspar van Baerle III. Zijn verder verblijf in Leiden. Vervolg' 248.
34 S.A.C. Dudok van Heel, *Van Amsterdamse burgers tot Europese aristocraten. Hun geschiedenis en hun portretten. De Heijnen-maagschap 1400-1800* (The Hague 2008), discusses the Libertarian faction of Bas, Bicker and De Graeff on page 177 and 185.
35 To complicate matters further, Alewijn had previously been married to Agatha Geelvinck, daughter of Jan Cornelis Geelvinck, another one of the burgomasters who appointed Barlaeus in 1629. See P.C. Molhuysen, P.J. Blok et al. (eds.), *Nieuw Nederlandsch Biografisch Woordenboek,* 10 vols., (Leiden and Amsterdam 1911–1937) vol. 4, 32. For Barlaeus' compositions, see Petit, *Bibliographische Lijst,* entries 48, 71.

Amsterdam to the city's burgomasters.[36] He probably did not receive any financial rewards for these poetic endeavours, in contrast to the ones he sent out to Frederick Henry; I have, at least, not found any reference to such rewards. Yet, his poems must have served to cement his new, comfortable position in Amsterdam.

Although Barlaeus expanded his network when moving to Amsterdam, he also remained firmly attached to his previous circle and continued to dedicate works to those associated with the court in The Hague.[37] In addition, he also published several works celebrating foreign rulers, and honoured two colleagues from his Leiden time with funeral orations.[38] Thus, Barlaeus' move to Amsterdam by no means resulted in a total severance of his previous friendships.

He finally set up house in Amsterdam in 1631. His home in the Spinhuissteeg was located near the Athenaeum Illustre (on the Oudezijds Voorburgwal), next to Vossius' house. A close friendship between the two men developed, and Barlaeus also found comfort in the presence of other learned men. Once classes started and Barlaeus established a routine of his own, he even

36 Petit, *Bibliographische Lijst*, entry 67.
37 On these friendships and dedications, see Worp, 'Caspar van Baerle IV. Eerste Jaren te Amsterdam' and 'Caspar van Baerle V. Zijn verder verblijf te Amsterdam (1635-1644)', *Oud-Holland*, vol. 6 (1888) 87-102. For correspondence regarding the efforts of Huygens, Van der Myle and Van Wicquefort to ensure Barlaeus' payment from Frederick Henry, see Blok, *From the Correspondence of a Melancholic* 56-60, 88, 90, 124-125, 155-156. On Schonck, see idem 91; Worp, 'Caspar van Baerle IV. Eerste Jaren te Amsterdam' 101 and Barlaeus to Constantijn Huygens, 23 July 1633, through *ePistolarium,* consulted 22 February 2017. Finally, Barlaeus also wrote a marriage poem for Katherine Wotton and Johannes Polyander van Kerckhoven Jr., another one of Frederick Henry's confidants, as well as for Walburg, Johannes' daughter of his first marriage. See Petit, *Bibliographische Lijst*, entries 76 and 91.
38 Barlaeus dedicated three works to foreign rulers: Gustav Adolf II of Sweden, prince-elect Christian of Denmark, and cardinal Richelieu; see Petit, *Bibliographische Lijst*, entries 45, 53 and 77. The Leiden colleagues Barlaeus honoured are Simon Episcopius – who, from 1634 onward, headed the Remonstrant seminary in Amsterdam – and Johannes Polyander van Kerckhoven Sr; Petit, *Bibliographische Lijst,* entries 83 and 93.

came to appreciate the city.[39] This appreciation turned out to be mutual: several sources indicate that Barlaeus was a valued professor at the Athenaeum, and the funerary oration delivered by his friend and colleague Corvinus not only recalled the strong bonds of friendship Barlaeus had formed, but also stressed how often, and how well, he had addressed his audience from the exact place Corvinus was speaking.[40]

Unfortunately, the fragile constitution that refrained Barlaeus from practising medicine would continue to influence his life and career. A few months after the Athenaeum had opened, Barlaeus fell ill. He wrote an old friend in Leiden that he had become 'melancholic', a disorder from which he had suffered before and which would continue to haunt him all his life. It was allegedly caused by an excessive presence of black bile, one of the four humours that were supposed to keep the body balanced. Barlaeus recovered reasonably quickly from the episode of 1632, but he experienced several more episodes near the end of his life. These may have been triggered by the personal drama that haunted Barlaeus after his move to Amsterdam: he lost several children, and in 1635 his wife Barbara died.[41] In the later stages of the disease, delusional ideas could also occur, and it is likely that Barlaeus ultimately died as a result of these: on 14 January 1648, just before the Athenaeum's morning classes would start, Barlaeus drowned in a rain-pit or well, possibly in an attempt to extinguish the imaginary fire his delusions made him see and feel.[42] Vossius was one of the first to know of his

39 Rademaker, *Life and Work of Gerard Vossius, 1577-1649* (Assen 1981) 240 and 246; Blok, *From the Correspondence of a Melancholic* 14-15. A description of the Agnietenkapel, in which the Athenaeum was housed, can be found in Van Miert, *Humanism in an Age of Science* 45. Vossius and Barlaeus would eventually both move to the Oudezijds Achterburgwal; Blok, *From the Correspondence of a Melancholic* 11.
40 Van Elslandt, *Lyk-Reden* 4, 16-18.
41 Worp, 'Caspar van Baerle IV. Eerste jaren te Amsterdam (1631-1635)' 111-112; Worp, 'Caspar van Baerle V. Zijn verder verblijf te Amsterdam' 87-88.
42 See Blok, *From the Correspondence of a Melancholic* 20-28, 155-184 for a more elaborate discussion of Barlaeus' illness and death.

Portrait of Caspar Barlaeus by Joachim von Sandrart, made between 1637 and 1643. Rijksmuseum, Amsterdam

friend, neighbour, and colleague's passing, and wrote his friend Pieter de Groot: 'Yesterday, at about the time when he was due to mount the rostrum, I was suddenly called by the children. But he had already breathed his last before I reached him.'[43]

The strange circumstances in which Barlaeus died spurred speculations of suicide, although not everyone chose to believe them. The rumours were made worse by the unexpectedness of Barlaeus' death. His acquaintances mentioned this fact in their letters; Corvinus called attention to it in his funerary oration (Vossius, the most obvious candidate to give the oration, had fallen ill) and the poems accompanying the published edition of Corvinus' speech also referred to it.[44] Celebrating the wide scope and high quality of Barlaeus' many publications, Corvinus said 'the world would have seen many more of his wonders' had it not been for his unexpected passing.[45] Of course, Corvinus did not neglect to speak words of admiration for Barlaeus' activities at the Athenaeum Illustre, and praised the scholar's diligence, erudition and passion for teaching: 'From this place, the deceased used to sharpen us with his wisdom: but alas! He will no longer sharpen us. You have, like me, heard him often when he showed his great passion, and affection toward us in his teaching; but you will hear him no more.'[46]

---

43 Vossius to Pieter de Groot, 15 January 1648, in Blok, *From the Correspondence of a Melancholic* 165-166 (transl. Blok).
44 Van Elslandt, *Lyk-Reden* 30-40; the poems were written by respectively Jacob Westerbaen, Joost van den Vondel, Gerard Brandt, Reyer Anslo and Van Elslandt, some of the Republic's most prominent poets.
45 Ibidem 20-21. Quote on p. 21: 'De Werelt soude meer wondren van hem ghesien hebben; maer syn leven was ten ende, de doodt heeft hem haestich wegh-gheruckt, een onderwachten hart-vangh benam hem 't leven, men hoorde dat hy 't leven verlaten hadde eer der een voor-boo van 't sterven was.'
46 Ibidem 4: 'Van dese plaets plach de overledene ons sijn wijsheyt in te scherpen; maer ach! hy sal se ons niet meer in scherpen. Gy hebt hem nevens my, als hy sijn groote drift, en genegentheyt t'ons waerts in 't onderwijsen betoonde, dickwils gehoort; maer ghy sult hem niet meer hooren.'

The Athenaeum Illustre

Barlaeus' death was all the more lamentable as he had made such a splendid impression the very first time he had mounted the rostrum. He addressed Amsterdam's elite, and praised them for their initiative to start an institution of higher learning in a city that had so far mostly been dedicated to the pursuit of earthly profits:

> Every time I look upon this city of yours – which is now my city as well – and let my gaze wander over all its marvellous sights, I deliberate as to what I should admire in it first, what second and what last. ... Nature and labour, virtue and fortune, earth and sea seem to have vied with each other to make this city great. All of this, however, although it is excellent, splendid and admirable, spreading at home and abroad the fame of a most prosperous city, should be considered less important than this project of the honourable council and burgomasters, by which on this day they begin to pursue a new jewel in their republic's crown in a manner that is new and unusual to this place: from the study of wisdom and literature, and public classes on these subjects.[47]

The city of Amsterdam had developed rapidly in the early decades of the seventeenth century. New neighbourhoods and splendid churches arose and the city became known as a capital of freedom and wealth. It assumed a prominent position in the province of Holland as well as in the Dutch Republic as a whole, and inspired admiration and jealousy in the rest of Europe. Yet, despite this new-found prosperity, the city lacked a university or institution of higher learning that would add lustre to its name and attract students from elsewhere.[48] The city did have several Latin schools,

---

47 Barlaeus, *The Wise Merchant* 73, 9-11 and 30-32, 75, 1-6.
48 Van Miert, *Humanism in an Age of Science* 28; Blok, *From the Correspondence of a Melancholic* 11-12.

which served the children of Amsterdam *burghers*, but these schools did not attract students from abroad, nor pupils from the other larger cities of the Republic, as these had their own Latin schools. For precisely this reason, these Latin schools did not improve Amsterdam's status: the city was in no way unique in this regard. Thus, the foundation of the Athenaeum Illustre was closely tied to the desire for intellectual recognition and Amsterdam's new-found prosperity.

The one institution of higher learning that would definitely attract students to the city and add lustre to its name was, of course, a university. Unfortunately for Amsterdam, however, Leiden had been granted the exclusive right to this illustrious institution in the provinces of Holland and Zeeland.[49] Amsterdam was permitted to open an Illustrious School, as several other cities had done before. Illustrious Schools did not have the right to grant academic degrees, making them less prestigious than universities, and usually provided pupils with the education necessary to bridge the gap between the Latin school and the university level. Their propaedeutic programme focused on the *artes liberales*.[50] And although not as impressive as a university, an Illustrious School would still increase Amsterdam's standing.[51]

In his oration, Barlaeus explicitly referred to the quest for prestige as a motive for the establishment of the Athenaeum Illustre. First, he asked God in the opening prayer for several things, among them intellectual renown: 'Grant us, most merciful God, that this city, so ample in territory, so busy with citizens, so renowned for its commerce, gain greater renown from the value of its learning.' Second, in the main body of the text Barlaeus explicitly argued that wealthy cities need institutes of learning: 'But all books and all Antiquity are full of examples from which we know that the wisest men already said as much in those times;

49   Van Miert, *Humanism in an Age of Science* 41.
50   Ibidem 32-34.
51   Ibidem 28.

Proceedings of the *vroedschap*-meeting on 31 December 1629, which led to the foundation of the Athenaeum Illustre and the appointment of Caspar Barlaeus. In the Vroedschapsresoluties, Gemeente-archief Amsterdam, Archive no. 5025, Index no. 93

that precisely the wealthiest cities cannot do without schools, teachers, libraries and the other instruments of wisdom.'[52]

Still, when the burgomasters and city council discussed the possible foundation of an Illustrious School in Amsterdam, a quest for prestige and status was not at the forefront of their minds. In their meeting of 31 December 1629, they mentioned the complaints they had received regarding the education of the city's youth. The burgomasters explained to the city council that when boys finished the Latin school in Amsterdam, they had to leave the city in order to pursue a university education elsewhere. According to the burgomasters, this was problematic for two reasons. First, the young boys were ill prepared for this step since they had not yet received proper education in the fundamentals of philosophy. Second, the young boys were exposed to a strange city and a rough student life at the age of sixteen, or sometimes even fourteen, without the supervision of their parents.[53]

The city council acknowledged the importance of the complaints right away and asked the burgomasters to look out for a suitable auditorium. They were also authorized to search for a learned and able person, whom they could install with the salary they saw fit.[54] This learned and able person was Barlaeus,

52 Barlaeus, *The Wise Merchant* 67, 16-18 and 113, 12-15. Vossius also mentioned the desire for prestige as an important motivation for the foundation of the Athenaeum Illustre in his correspondence; see C.L. Heesakkers, 'Foundation and early development of the Athenaeum Illustre at Amsterdam', *Lias*, vol. 9, no. I (1982) 4.

53 Heesakkers, 'Athenaeum Illustre' 4; Van Miert, *Humanism in an Age of Science* 40. In 1629, the burgomasters were Jan Cornelisz Geelvinck, Abraham Boom, Anthonie Oetgens van Waveren and Andries Bicker. Barlaeus dedicated the printed edition of his oration to the latter two, as well as to Jacob de Graeff, Dirck Bas and Jan Grotenhuys. These five men formed the head of the city council in 1631; De Graef, Bas, Oetgens van Waveren and Bicker were burgomasters, and Grotenhuys *schout*. In addition, they were the Athenaeum's first curators. See *Beschryvinge van Amsterdam, haar eerste oorspronk uyt den huyze der heeren van Aemstel en Aemstellant: met een verhaal van haar leven en dappere krijgsdaden* (Amsterdam 1665) 478, available on Google Books.

54 Heesakkers, 'Athenaeum Illustre' 4; Van Miert, *Humanism in an Age of Science* 40.

who at the time still resided in Leiden. It is likely, however, that he had even been approached *before* the official meeting of the city council: in a letter written on 31 December 1629, the same day the city council convened, Barlaeus wrote an acquaintance that he 'had heard, here and there, that this rumour circulates with persistence, at least among persons who this issue does not concern. Whether something about me has been decided, I cannot yet determine for lack of trustworthy spokesmen.'[55] From this letter it appears that the idea to establish an Illustrious School had originated somewhat earlier, and that informal preparations had already started before the city council gave the official order. Yet it still took two full years before the Athenaeum actually opened.

This delay had nothing to do with Barlaeus, who quickly accepted the burgomasters' offer, regardless of the doubts he voiced to his correspondents. The offer was simply too good to reject. In April 1630, informal inquiries were made again: this time to ask whether Vossius would be interested in becoming the second professor of the Illustrious School. This would prevent a complete standstill in case of illness. In December 1630, the city council formalized its decision to employ two persons. In light of Barlaeus' melancholic episodes, this turned out to be a wise decision: Barlaeus already fell ill in the first months of his appointment, leaving Vossius as sole professor for several weeks.[56]

Barlaeus and Vossius visited Amsterdam in January 1631 to look at housing prospects, but Vossius only accepted the Athenaeum's job offer in August. He was in a different position: although both men had been fired from the Statencollege, Vossius had later been

---

55 Translation mine, after Heesakkers' ('Athenaeum Illustre' 4-5) Dutch translation. For the original Latin, see Heesakkers, 'Foundation and early development of the Athenaeum Illustre at Amsterdam' 4-5.

56 Heesakkers, 'Athenaeum Illustre' 4-5; C.S.M. Rademaker, 'De vrijdom ga sijn' gang' in Heesakkers et al., *Vossius en Barlaeus: Twee helden die der dingen diept en steilt'afpeilen. Het Athenaeum Illustre en zijn eerste hoogleraren* (Amsterdam 1982) 12-23, 13.

appointed Professor of Rhetoric and Greek at the University of Leiden.[57] He was not immediately prepared to leave this comfortable position and wanted insurances that his workload would not increase and his salary would not decrease. The Athenaeum offered him the exceptionally high salary of 2,600 guilders, as well as many benefits including housing and a widow's pension. The decisive incentive might have been the more liberal atmosphere in Amsterdam: Vossius expected to finally have the time and freedom to publish works about theology and church history, which he had refrained from in Leiden.[58]

Vossius' potential departure from Leiden may have spurred the city to finally take formal action against Amsterdam's plans. Fearing that a large part of their potential students would prefer Amsterdam, they filed a complaint against the Athenaeum Illustre with the Court of Holland and Zeeland on 6 June 1631 – two months before Vossius officially accepted the Athenaeum's offer. Leiden's main claim was that the new school in Amsterdam would violate its exclusive privilege to a university. Amsterdam argued that it merely wished to offer education bridging the Latin School and the university, without providing schooling in theology, law and medicine. Although these promises were later broken, in December 1631 the court ruled in favour of Amsterdam. The city's lawyer had argued that it did not plan to open a competing university, but rather an institution that would prepare Amsterdam's youth for their Leiden university education. The court of Holland and Zeeland judged this a fair claim and granted Amsterdam its Illustrious School.[59] Their

---

57   Rademaker, *Life and Work of Gerard Vossius* xxvi, chapter 3, section 3 (esp. 125-142) and chapter 3, section I (143-166). Also Van Netten, *Koopman in Kennis* 191-192 and Rademaker, "De vrijdom ga sijn' gang" 13-14.
58   Rademaker, "De vrijdom ga sijn gang" 13; Rademaker, *Life and Work* 238 and 310.
59   P.C. Molhuysen, *Bronnen tot de geschiedenis der Leidsche Universiteit,* 5 vols., (The Hague 1913-1924) vol. 2, 153-155, 159, 214*-252*, 285*-289*. Asterisks refer to page numbers in the Appendices. A discussion of the conflict, based on these sources, can be found in W. Frijhoff, 'Het Amsterdamse Athenaeum in het academische

Portrait of Gerard Vossius by David Bailly, 1624. Rijksmuseum, Amsterdam

landschap van de zeventiende eeuw' in E.O.G. Haitsma Mulier, C.L. Heesakkers, P.J. Knegtmans, A.J. Kox and T.J. Veen (eds.), *Athenaeum Illustre. Elf studies over de Amsterdamse Doorlluchtige School 1632-1877* (Amsterdam 1997) 37-65, 61-65.

View of the Athenaeum Illustre on the Oudezijds Voorburgwal, anonymous, 1663–1665. Rijksmuseum, Amsterdam

main argument was that the Athenaeum would not compete directly with Leiden as it was not allowed to award doctorates.[60]

Three weeks later, the Athenaeum was in business and not one, but two learned and able persons delivered their inaugural oration from the rostrum at the Oudezijds Voorburgwal.[61] With Barlaeus and Vossius, the burgomasters had attracted two scholars of great renown to enhance Amsterdam's status, and they were welcomed accordingly. On 2 May, the day after Barlaeus arrived in the city, the *schout* (sherriff) Jan Grootenhuys came to his home to welcome him to Amsterdam.[62] The city council could count themselves lucky with their new professors. Barlaeus had gained international fame through his writings, while later sources would praise his didactic skills as well.[63] Vossius ranked even higher than Barlaeus: the differences in salary as well as the fact that his opening oration took place the day before Barlaeus', are clear signs of the hierarchy between the two men.[64] More generally, there is no question that both men were well suited to serve the Athenaeum as their inaugural addresses also showed.

Apart from the two practical arguments described in the council's minutes, and the quest for intellectual renown, the city council and the burgomasters may have had a fourth reason to start the Athenaeum Illustre: it would allow their own sons to receive an education that would prepare them for their public careers in the new political climate of the Dutch Republic. Studying ancient history, rhetoric and philosophy would enable them to learn from the illustrious history of the Greeks and Romans

60 Blok, *From the Correspondence of a Melancholic* 13-14. Van Miert has argued this difference existed mostly in theory, as students could easily obtain a doctorate at a different university by briefly enrolling rather than completing an entire course of study. Towards 1700, furthermore, the Athenaeum had appointed professors in law, theology and medicine as well. In Van Miert, *Humanism in an Age of Science* 40-42, 110.

61 Heesakkers, 'Athenaeum Illustre' 6.

62 Worp, 'Caspar van Baerle. Eerste Jaren te Amsterdam' 93.

63 Blok, 'Caspar Barlaeus, de filosoof van het Athenaeum Illustre' in Rademaker et al., *Twee Helden* 24-32, 26; Blok, *From the Correspondence of a Melancholic* 10-11.

64 Van Miert, *Humanism in an Age of Science* 4.

and grasp the ancient principles of good government.[65] Their sons would not be the only ones benefiting from this type of education. The two professors would deliver their lectures each morning from 9.00 to 10.00 (Barlaeus) and from 10.00 to 11.00 (Vossius), thus enabling Amsterdam's merchants to attend their classes before going to the Exchange, which was open from 11.00 to 12.00 each day.[66]

Barlaeus and Vossius adapted their opening lectures to this type of public, to convince them of the use and importance of the new-found Athenaeum. Both men, therefore, spoke on the utility of their own subjects: Barlaeus on the use of philosophy, Vossius on the use of history. Both speakers emphasized the relevance of their subject: Vossius by arguing that life is too short to learn everything by oneself, and that the shortest and most practical way to knowledge is history.[67] Barlaeus appealed specifically to the merchants in the audience, and stressed the relevance of trade for the city of Amsterdam. As such, his choice of subject matter was especially apt, as Corvinus also signalled in his funerary oration.[68]

It is likely that Barlaeus and Vossius coordinated their efforts to reach out to Amsterdam's ruling and mercantile elite, both in their opening speeches and in the lectures to follow. In a letter to Huygens, Barlaeus discussed both inaugural speeches, and mentioned they were now at the publisher to be printed. He then told Huygens of the first regular lectures the two of them had given:

> After the speeches we began our lectures, Vossius on the time from the creation of the world until the time of Abraham, I on the schools and tenets of the ancient philosophers, the

65   Ibidem 22-24, 354, 358.
66   Blok, 'Caspar Barlaeus' 27; Worp, 'Caspar van Baerle IV. Eerste Jaren te Amsterdam' 96-97.
67   Rademaker, *Life and Work of Gerard Vossius* 242-243.
68   Van Elslandt, *Lyk-Reden* 21.

Academics, the Stoics, the Epicureans and the Peripatetics. It is our intention that the merchants take to the taste of it and that we arouse in them a love for these studies, from which they have until now held themselves at some considerable distance. The start conforms with our wishes; but I fear that here again it will be proved that the beginning is hot etc.[69]

Although Barlaeus initially felt that his and Vossius' efforts to win the merchants for their cause had been successful, he also feared they might not be able to maintain their interest. It is hard to say whether his intuition was correct, as it is impossible to determine which – or how many – people attended Vossius' and Barlaeus' lectures in the following years. Even enrolment numbers of regular students are difficult to establish, let alone the irregular attendance of non-enrolled merchants or administrators.[70] Several letters, written by the two professors or their acquaintances, indicate that their lectures were popular and drew the attention of the merchants. Yet, these also suggest that they occasionally had to adjust the subject of their lectures. Vossius, for instance, told his correspondent William Boswell he had to shift the focus of his lectures to Roman history rather than Church history. Otherwise, he – and the Athenaeum – ran the risk of attracting fewer students, who would no longer come to the 'lesson market'.[71]

69   Barlaeus to Huygens from 18 January 1632, in Blok, *From the Correspondence of a Melancholic* 17. With 'The beginning is hot etc.' Barlaeus quotes a medieval proverb: 'The beginning is hot, the middle tepid, the end cold', again in Blok, *From the Correspondence of a Melancholic* 17, n41. Vossius wrote Johannes Corvinus that his lecture had also been successful, and had drawn a large and varied audience, see Wilhelmina G. Kamerbeek, 'Some Letters by Johannes Arnoldi Corvinus', *Lias* vol. 9, no. 1 (1982) 93.
70   Van Miert, *Humanism in an Age of Science* 5; Frijhoff, 'Het Amsterdamse Athenaeum' 38-41.
71   Van Miert, *Humanism in an Age of Science* 194. See Rademaker, *Life and Work of Gerard Vossius* 244-245; Rademaker, 'The Athenaeum Illustre in the correspondence of Gerardus Johannes Vossius', *Lias* vol. 9, no. 1 (1982) 19-55, 33 for correspondence regarding the attendance of the lectures.

Interior of the Athenaeum Illustre in Amsterdam, possibly by Hermanus Petrus Schouten, c.1770–1783. Rijksmuseum, Amsterdam

It is clear that the Athenaeum prospered with Barlaeus and Vossius in charge.[72] Within a decade after its opening, the Athenaeum established two new chairs – Martinus Hortensius started his lectures in mathematics in 1634, while Johannes Cabeliau was appointed Professor of Law in 1640 – and even tried to attract the famous Italian mathematician Galileo Galilei.[73] This attempt failed – Galileo did not wish to leave Italy at his old age –, and not all professors hired after Barlaeus' and Vossius' deaths in 1648 and 1649 would prove as learned and able as they had been. Although this hurt the Athenaeum's status, no serious problems arose until the beginning of the eighteenth century, when economic decline and declining enrolment numbers in the Dutch Republic as a whole coincided with staffing problems at

72 Rademaker, *Life and Work of Gerard Vossius* 245.
73 Van Miert, *Humanism in an Age of Science* 55-60.

the Athenaeum Illustre.[74] Nonetheless, the Athenaeum remained in business until it was given the status of an official university in 1877. From that moment onwards, it would be known as the University of Amsterdam.[75] The names of its two first professors would, from 1927, be attached to two other institutes of learning in the city: the Barlaeus Gymnasium and the Vossius Gymnasium, which provide high school education – including Greek and/or Latin – to boys and girls between the ages of twelve and eighteen.

The oration

The oration Barlaeus delivered on 9 January 1632 has come down to us in its printed version, published by Willem Jansz. Blaeu. This edition is dedicated to the Athenaeum's curators: the four burgomasters who ruled Amsterdam in 1631, Anthonie Oetgens van Waveren, Andries Bicker, Jacob de Graeff and Dirck Bas, and to Jan Grootenhuys, the 'praetor' or *schout*: the highest magistrate in the city government.[76] Two of them, Oetgens van Waveren and Bicker, had also been in office when the Athenaeum was founded in 1629, and had invited Barlaeus to come to Amsterdam as its first professor. These men are excellent examples of the ways the mercantile and political elite of the city overlapped: all of them came from wealthy merchant families with long traditions of political power, and all of them had served as burgomasters before. Their family histories also illustrated the risks inherent

74   Ibidem 68, 110-111.
75   Ibidem 3.
76   The burgomasters were elected on the first of February and appointed for one year; those appointed in 1631 were therefore still in office in January, when Barlaeus held his oration. See M. Hell, 'De Oude Geuzen en de Opstand. Politiek en lokaal bestuur in tijd van oorlog en expansie 1578-1650' in W. Frijhoff and M. Prak (eds.), *Geschiedenis van Amsterdam. Centrum van de Wereld 1578-1650* (Amsterdam 2004) 241-297, 242. For more on these men, see J.E. Elias, *De Vroedschap van Amsterdam 1578-1795* (Amsterdam 1963), no. 84 (Grotenhuys), 80 (De Graef), 76 (Bas), 107 (Oetgens van Waveren) and 110 (Bicker).

to this overlap: with several others, Oetgens van Waveren's father had abused his power to greatly enrich himself during the 1612 expansion of Amsterdam. This led to a temporary lapse of his faction's power in 1615, although it managed to return to power in 1621.[77] These were the sort of men Barlaeus addressed in his oration, and knowing their background makes his frequent warnings and exhortations even more pungent.

Barlaeus spoke for approximately one hour: the printed edition of the oration consists of about 6,000 words, and Barlaeus' regular lectures took the same time. To retain his public's attention, Barlaeus addressed them directly at several points throughout the oration. Although we cannot establish with any certainty who attended the opening, Barlaeus explicitly addressed different groups of people in his oration as if they were present at the time. The city government, the city's ministers, its merchants and traders, and its youth are all called upon, and enticed to listen to Barlaeus' oration with arguments specifically suited to their interests and situation. What is more, Barlaeus' oration also contains implicit or explicit calls to action for each of these groups: the ministers, for instance, are called upon to prevent further religious strife, while the civil government is asked to serve and support learning rather than trade. Yet taken together, the arguments presented in the oration serve one overarching aim: to raise interest in and goodwill for the Athenaeum Illustre as an institute of learning in the city, dedicated to the study of the ancients. Within this overarching and seemingly harmonious framework, three important themes deserve further attention. An analysis of the oration based on these themes not only improves our understanding of Barlaeus' ideas on each individual topic, but also increases our grasp on the oration as a whole.

---

77   See Dudok van Heel, *Van Amsterdamse burgers tot Europese aristocraten*; Elias, *De Vroedschap van Amsterdam*; and Lesger, *Handel in Amsterdam*, 142-144 on the links between the political and the mercantile elites in Amsterdam. Lesger discusses the misconduct of Frans Hendricksz Oetgens and others between 1612-1615 on pages 171-172.

The first of these is the relation between the roles of the government of Amsterdam and the Reformed Church. Although Barlaeus opens his oration with a prayer, the secular government consistently comes before the Church in the remainder of the text. The clearest example of this hierarchy can already be found in the opening prayer preceding the oration, when Barlaeus lists those present: 'Before you stands the supplicant republic [...]. Before you stands the supplicant church [...]. Before you stands the supplicant citizenry [...] Before you stands the supplicant youth [...]'.[78] In these first few sentences, the hierarchy that continues throughout the oration is immediately established: republic before church. This pattern is repeated at several points in the oration.[79] As Secretan pointed out, this is how Barlaeus firmly places himself in the Remonstrant tradition of valuing the authority of the state over the Church.[80] We also detect his experience as a Remonstrant in his appeal to God to unite those divided by faith: 'Gather together the members of your church that were torn apart, so that those who were separated by diversity of opinions may be united by a prevailing love. Bind the citizens in mutual love and banish all causes of dispute from these city walls.'[81]

Judging from the examples cited above, Barlaeus' text should not be considered as completely secular: he consistently puts the Church in second place and does not exclude it entirely. The same is true for the role of Christian teaching in the oration. As Van der Woude's edition shows, many Biblical references can be found throughout the main body of the text. These are not as prominently presented as references to ancient authors; not only are there far fewer references to the Bible, these references are also less explicitly announced to the public. Whereas Barlaeus often explicitly introduces ancient quotes or sayings, he leaves references to the Bible implicit. This may, at least partly, be explained by the

78 Barlaeus, *The Wise Merchant* 67, 5-13.
79 Ibidem, see for instance page 69 and 119.
80 Secretan, *Le 'Marchand Philosophe'* 72-75; Prak, *The Dutch Republic* 30.
81 Barlaeus, *The Wise Merchant* 69, 25-29.

familiarity of his public with Biblical teaching, as opposed to their knowledge of the ancients. Of course, promoting the latter was also an integral part of Barlaeus' oration: by showing the relevance of ancient knowledge to current-day affairs, he hoped to reel in his audience and spur their enthusiasm for the Athenaeum Illustre.[82]

This brings us to a second important theme, namely the relation between ancient and modern knowledge. The influence of ancient rhetoric is notable in the form and structure of the text, but the importance Barlaeus assigned to ancient wisdom becomes most clear from the more than 150 references to ancient writers and works. The oration similarly contains several references to humanist authors.[83] These references serve not only to legitimize Barlaeus' subject matter, but also to present authoritative examples. Barlaeus further derived lessons from the teachings of ancient authors with regard to the proper way of conducting trade. Moral philosophy, especially through the teachings of the Stoics, teaches merchants how to trade and live wisely, whereas speculative philosophy serves as a more practical guide. In this sense, Barlaeus' text is more conservative than it is sometimes made out to be: it presents a clear case for the study of the ancients, rather than advocate 'the new science', as Harold Cook has argued.[84]

Barlaeus did not only rely on ancient authorities to make his case. He also cited Erasmus, 'immortal ornament of our Holland' as a fervent admirer of Cicero, thus presenting his public with an example of another Christian, Dutch humanist they might follow. Barlaeus thus not only gave his public one more legitimation of the importance of ancient authors – Cicero in particular – but also highlighted the importance of the Dutch intellectual tradition.

82 On Barlaeus' treatment of Christian and ancient teaching, also see Van der Woude, *Mercator Sapiens* 14-15 who has argued that the Church plays no role in the main body in the text. It is only mentioned in the opening prayer preceding the oration, and the Church Fathers are dismissed in favour of the ancient philosophers near the end of the oration.

83 Van der Woude, *Mercator Sapiens* 15.

84 See notes 10 and 11 above.

At different points throughout the oration, Barlaeus presents Amsterdam as the heir to the traditions of Athens, Sparta and Rome.[85] He also reinforces this argument by stressing the intellectual importance of the Dutch Republic through citing its most famous exponent, Erasmus.[86]

The most important theme of the oration is the triumph of wisdom over trade. Although Barlaeus' oration is devoted to the combination of the pursuits of wisdom and trade, this combination is not without friction, and it is not a union on equal terms. Early in the oration, a hierarchy between the two clearly manifests itself to those who listen carefully and who perhaps even notice the warnings Barlaeus includes in his oration. Throughout the oration, Barlaeus stresses time and time again that trade without wisdom is worthless, and might even lead

85 Presenting a city or state as the successor of ancient Rome or Athens was a *topos* employed by many different cities in early modern Europe. See W. Velema and A. Weststeijn (eds.), *Ancient Models in the Early Modern Republican Imagination* (Leiden and Boston 2017) for a recent exploration of the importance of ancient models in early modern Europe.

86 Although the Dutch author Dirck Volkertsz. Coornhert (1522-1590) is not explicitly discussed in Barlaeus' oration, his work is often compared to Barlaeus' in recent literature. Coornhert, who was born in Amsterdam and the scion of a merchant family, wrote extensively on ethical questions, and his exploration of the way merchants should behave resulted in a short work titled *De Coopman: Aenwysende d'oprechte conste om Christelyck ende met eenen gelycken moede in 't winnen ende verliesen coophandel te dryven* (Norden 1580). This work, written in 1580, took the form of a dialogue between the fictive character of Gerard Mercator and Coornhert himself. Although familiar with Ciceronian philosophy – Coornhert had translated *De Officiis* in the 1560s – Coornhert's advice to merchants was almost entirely based on Christian principles, while Barlaeus' reasoning is clearly rooted in ancient philosophy. See Weststeijn, *Commercial Republicanism* 188-190; Secretan, *Le 'Marchand Philosophe'* 81-90; and Lis and Soly, *Worthy Efforts* 263 for a more extensive discussion of Coornhert and Barlaeus. Lis and Soly, as well as K. Bostoen, 'Zo eerlijk als goud: de ethiek van de wereldstad' in H. Pleij (ed.), *Op belofte van profijt. Stadsliteratuur en burgermoraal in de Nederlandse letterkunde van de middeleeuwen* (Amsterdam 1991) 333-346, also discuss how the topic of virtuous trade was taken up by the Chambers of Rhetoric, especially during the 1561 edition of the Antwerp *Landjuweel*-festival, where different groups of *rederijkers* each presented a literary discussion of the importance of good merchants.

to ruin. Those who possess true wisdom, on the other hand, do not desire wealth, as they realize its ephemeral character will not bring them joy. As this message is wrapped in flattery and arguments that seemingly advocate trade, many listeners might just have thought Barlaeus fully endorsed their activities – as has been the outcome of several later interpretations of the oration.[87] Yet, a closer look at the text as a whole reveals Barlaeus' much more reserved stance on this matter. This becomes especially clear if we follow Barlaeus' argument from the start of the oration.

Following the opening prayer, the text contains a brief panegyric of the city of Amsterdam, and states that the speaker does not know what to praise first when looking around: Amsterdam's churches? Its poor houses? The towers and lighthouses? Its dams and sluices, or the merchant's porticos? The expensive goods that are brought into the city, or the ships carrying them, or perhaps the ports in which they land? The splendour of the buildings, or the magnitude of the crowds? The observance of prudence of the regents and the observance of the law, or perhaps the obedience of the subjects, their modesty and their orderliness? No; although each of these elements are admirable and praiseworthy in themselves, none of them are as admirable as the initiative started by the city council: to found the Athenaeum Illustre. For the riches the Athenaeum brings are eternal, and will survive all of Amsterdam's fleeting material wealth.

It was, Barlaeus continued, indeed appropriate that this city, which abounded in worldly treasures, had finally started thinking about the benefits of immortality. This, he emphasized, was something new to Amsterdam, as the city had so far been mainly concerned with the acquisition of worldly wealth. For that reason, it would be useless to speak about anything else than commerce,

---

87 See for instance: Lis and Soly, *Worthy Efforts* 264: 'His speech was one long ode to businessmen, without any reservations and in some places giving highly creative interpretations of historical facts'; Secretan, *Le 'Marchand Philosophe'* 55: 'It is by conferring on the entire merchant profession, as a whole, the nobility of an activity comparable to that of philosophy that [Barlaeus] intends to irrefutably establish the dignity of trade.'

profit and wealth. He immediately admitted that he did not think he could teach Amsterdam's inhabitants how to make a profit. He could, however, teach them how to do it wisely. Here, we encounter Barlaeus' double-edged message for the first time: he added that he did not want 'to condemn the pursuit of wealth, but to keep it in check with the brake of reason'.[88] In other words: just after promising to teach merchants how to trade wisely, Barlaeus immediately added he would actually show them how to *temper* their pursuit of wealth.

He followed these remarks with a brief outline of his main argument:

> This I will show: that trade and the pursuit of wisdom and the arts go together very well, and that neither the care for augmenting one's wealth is in the way of the mind's contemplations, nor vice versa. On the contrary, the human faculty for trade and that for philosophy work together in the best of ways: the more splendidly a merchant can philosophize, the luckier I will deem him.[89]

In these few sentences, both Barlaeus' argument and his rhetorical strategy become crystal clear. Although he first suggested that trade and the pursuit of wisdom go together very well and positively impact each other, the next statement shows that the relation between the two is not an equal one. Barlaeus praises the merchant who philosophizes, but not the philosopher who trades.

He subsequently gives several examples which show the importance assigned to philosophy and trade in Antiquity. Barlaeus shows that trade and wisdom had helped each other since Antiquity; that the antiquity of trade is best studied based on the works of the ancient philosophers, and that the link between trade and philosophy is a suitable subject for an oration. Left implicit is the fact that although the ancient authors Barlaeus mentions

88 Barlaeus, *The Wise Merchant* 77, 19-20.
89 Ibidem 77, 20-26.

did recognize a link between trade and philosophy, most of the stories he recounts in the oration actually contained the clear lesson that although trade may benefit from philosophy, the latter always triumphs over trade. The exception may be found in his opening statement, where Barlaeus presents an actual argument for the benefit of trade for wisdom, derived from Antiquity: 'these two pursuits have always benefited one another, as the wise have always believed that it was impossible to solve human problems without exchanging merchandise, and on the other hand it is well known that through such an exchange, big steps are made towards prudence.'[90] Barlaeus found an argument in favour of trade in its usefulness to society: the exchange of goods also leads to an exchange of ideas and an understanding of foreign people.

In the subsequent discussion of the ancient writings on trade and wisdom, two examples stand out. The first one concerns his discussion of the marketplace as envisioned by Pythagoras:

> Even Pythagoras, who came before Plato, distinguished the entire marketplace into three types of people: those who had come to sell, those who had come to buy – both these types, he said, are agitated and consequently less fortunate – and the third type, who come to the market merely to watch, the only type he named fortunate, because without worries they enjoy a free pleasure.[91]

Here, Barlaeus again applied a clear hierarchy: while seemingly advocating trade, he actually only makes a case for philosophy, as those who do not participate in the marketplace and only study it from a distance, are the happiest. This, it seems, is what he hoped the Athenaeum's students would learn to do.[92]

---

90   Ibidem 79, 9-13.
91   Ibidem 81, 21-27.
92   S. Rauschenbach, 'Elzevirian Republics, Wise Merchants, and New Perspectives on Spain and Portugal in the Seventeenth-century Dutch Republic', *De Zeventiende Eeuw*, vol. 29, no. 1 (2013) 81-100, 87 draws the same conclusion.

After reciting several more examples of ancient authors discussing the unity of trade and wisdom, Barlaeus also presents his public with a coveted warning. By briefly recalling the story of Damasippus, who only turned to philosophy *after* going bankrupt, Barlaeus sent a clear message to those people in the audience who were arrogant enough to think they could do without philosophy: eventually, they would encounter ruin, and then it would be too late.[93] According to Barlaeus, these examples showed 'that the greatest men of learning and wisdom recognized a link between trade and philosophy, as between all the other arts, and spoke seriously of the very things we are now discussing.'[94]

How philosophy is beneficial to trade is dealt with in the next section of the oration, which starts with the following devilish statement: 'But I would like to consider the virtues of merchants more closely and demonstrate with some serious precepts borrowed from philosophy how wisdom can also remedy their shortcomings.'[95] The arguments presented in this part of the oration can be placed in the Stoic school of thought and amount to three important conclusions regarding the importance of philosophy to trade.[96] First, moral philosophy teaches merchants that they should actually not care about trade, as philosophy will make them realize wealth has very little value compared to knowledge. The philosopher would teach the merchant that one may only be considered rich if one stops desiring: a man's value should be measured by his way of life and culture, not by his wealth. Should the merchant follow this line of thought to the extreme, he would give up his business and take up the scholarly life. Barlaeus did not dwell on this argument but only presented it very briefly; speaking for an audience of merchants, he realized this message would not be favourably received. This

93 Barlaeus, *The Wise Merchant* 83-85.
94 Ibidem 85, 5-7.
95 Ibidem 85, 8-10.
96 For a more detailed discussion of how Barlaeus' oration relates to Stoic, Aristotelian and Ciceronian thinking, see Van Miert, *Humanism in an Age of Science* 226-228; and Weststeijn, *Commercial Republicanism* 185-190.

is, however, the overarching argument framing his oration, and it is implicitly present in the remainder of the text.

The second argument was more realistic: from moral philosophy, his public would also learn how to trade *wisely*. Apart from tempering their desire for riches, merchants should use their wealth to serve the common good. In other words: even if one has achieved riches, one should not let this determine one's character. Wealth should not inspire jealousy or greed, but should be put to use to further the glory of God and help one's neighbour and the poor. In that case, merchants may be considered truly virtuous: 'Wisdom does not despise the well-to-do, but approves of them especially: of those, that is, who are affluent without harming anyone, magnificent without decadence, generous without ostentation, serious without being morose, religious without superstition.'[97]

The link between wealth and virtue becomes most clear when Barlaeus describes the wise merchant and the relation between his wealth and his virtue in more concrete terms:

> When he looks closely at his coins, he imagines that piety is stamped onto one, honesty onto another, faith onto another, onto another prudence, kindness onto yet another, and in the very incentives to evil he imagines pictures of what is honourable. So when he lays aside whole stacks of money, it is as if he has laid aside the whole chorus of virtues as well.[98]

This was not an uncommon line of thought in the Dutch Republic: the wealthy grain merchant and multiple-time burgomaster Cornelis Pieterszoon Hooft felt that wealth reflected a man's personal qualities, and that wealthy men were wise, sensible and competent.[99] According to Barlaeus, the wise merchant is further inspired to act virtuously by his wealth in the realization that he

---

97   Barlaeus, *The Wise Merchant* 89, 13-17.
98   Ibidem 89, 22-28.
99   Lesger, 'Merchants in Charge' 81.

has been favoured by God and understands the responsibility that comes with his own fortune. Barlaeus stressed that his public consisted of such wise merchants, and with these statements perhaps implored them to share yet more of their wealth.[100]

He then moved on to the third characteristic of the wise merchant: he trades honourably and does not deceive others. Here, Barlaeus relied heavily on the teachings of Cicero and used an example from his work to illustrate what it means to trade wisely. Cicero, in *On Duties*, raised the following question: if a merchant sailing from Alexandria to Rhodes knows the price of grain in Rhodes is very high due to a shortage, may he sell his grain for the highest price, even if he knows more grain is on its way and the price will thus plunge soon? Although Cicero had other philosophers – such as Diogenes of Babylon[101] – argue that the merchant is not obliged to share his information by law and may, therefore, negotiate the best price possible, he himself stated that a merchant who knows more than a buyer and uses this to negotiate a better price, acts dishonourably. In his view, merchants are, like every other human being, bound to serve public welfare.[102] They should, therefore, share the information

---

100 Barlaeus, *The Wise Merchant* 89, 18-19.
101 Barlaeus, *The Wise Merchant* 97. Cicero's work contains an imaginary dialogue between Diogenes of Babylon and Antipater of Tarsus, which ultimately leads him to the conclusion the merchant should share the information with the starving population of Rhodes, see Lis and Soly, *Worthy Efforts* 224.
102 Cicero, *On duties*, III 52: "'What say you?' comes Antipater's argument on the other side; "it is your duty to consider the interests of your fellow men and to serve society; you were brought into the world under these conditions and have these inborn principles which you are in duty bound to obey and follow, that your interest shall be the interest of the community and conversely that the interest of the community shall be your interest as well". Barlaeus follows Cicero closely: 'Cicero on the other hand, together with the very sharp-witted philosopher Antipater, states that the information should not be concealed, because you are born under the law that you should not obstruct public welfare and as a human being should do well by other human beings, and as a citizen by fellow-citizens.' Barlaeus, *The Wise Merchant* 97, 18-23.

they have with the inhabitants of Rhodes, even if this means a decrease in profit.[103]

Barlaeus explicitly underlined the importance of ancient learning by adapting examples to fit the Dutch context. Hence, the Alexandrian merchant becomes a man from France, while Rhodes turns into Amsterdam.[104] He further used this concrete case to connect with his public by appealing to them directly: 'I think you understand that it is not just you, but also the ancient Romans who like sincerity, simplicity, candour, and who dislike cunning and deceit.'[105] This direct appeal enabled him to explicitly stress the utility and importance of ancient learning for modern Amsterdam and its inhabitants.

Thirdly, Barlaeus also argued for the utility of philosophy to trade on a different front altogether: philosophy may also help the merchant make such a profit. It is, however, not moral philosophy but speculative philosophy that does so. Speculative philosophy, as Barlaeus told his audience, comprises a broad array of disciplines, ranging from astronomy and mathematics to geology and ethnography. These subjects are more practically oriented and help the merchant with his enterprises abroad: he should learn to navigate the seas, as well as how to deal with foreign people.[106] Yet, this did not mean that the Athenaeum was teaching 'the new science', as Harold Cook phrased it: experimental philosophy had no place in the curriculum. Barlaeus here again leans heavily on ancient authors such as Aristotle, Pliny and Strabo, and promoted the study of ancient writers as part of the Athenaeum's curriculum.[107]

103 Barlaeus, *The Wise Merchant* 97-99.
104 See M. Spies, 'De Koopman van Rhodos. Over de schakelpunten van economie en cultuur', *De Zeventiende Eeuw* 6 (1990), 166-173 for a more elaborate discussion of Cicero's example in Barlaeus' oration, as well as in several other works.
105 Barlaeus, *The Wise Merchant* 99, 6-8.
106 Van Berkel, 'Rediscovering Clusius' 233.
107 Ibidem, 233; Van Miert, *Humanism in an Age of Science* 227-228; Weststeijn, *Commercial Republicanism* 187.

In sum, Barlaeus argued for the use of philosophy for trade on three different levels. First, it would teach merchants that they should actually not care about trade – an argument that probably did not find much traction with most of his public, but that Barlaeus, as a true humanist scholar, made anyway. Second, as he knew his public would not agree with the first argument, he also argued that philosophy would teach them how to trade wisely. This argument must have pleased Amsterdam's political-mercantile elite, especially as it emphasized their own virtues and offered them a (partial) intellectual legitimation of their pursuits. Finally, he argued speculative philosophy would help them further increase their wealth.

As both moral and speculative philosophy would be taught at the Athenaeum Illustre, we may conclude that Barlaeus argued for the use of the newly opened school on these three grounds. Seen in this light, and taking Barlaeus' consistent dismissal of trade as a pursuit equal to that of wisdom into account, it is perfectly possible to see the oration as a plea for wisdom and the Athenaeum Illustre, rather than as one praising the union of wisdom and trade on equal terms. Indeed, we may view the text in its entirety as an elaborate *captatio benevolentiae* for the Athenaeum Illustre.[108] By choosing a topic so important to his powerful public, and by seemingly flattering the men in his audience while simultaneously proclaiming them insufficiently cultured, Barlaeus managed to achieve a perfect balance, superbly suited to his purpose. On the one hand, he subtly told his public that, although they were already quite virtuous, they had not *quite* reached the level of moral virtue they should aspire to. On the other hand, he promised them this higher level was within their reach: through study of the ancients, under his own auspices at the school they had recently financed, they might yet achieve true wisdom.

---

108 Van Miert, *Humanism in an Age of Science* 228: 'Barlaeus knew exactly how to pitch a clever *captatio benevolentiae*'.

Thus, Barlaeus delivered what he had promised in the opening paragraphs and managed to reel in his public with this 'enticing bait'. Rather than legitimizing the merchant's active participation on the world stage through the lessons of the ancients as well as of recent, Erasmian humanism, the oration legitimized the pursuit of ancient knowledge on moral and practical grounds.[109] This conclusion is supported by the final paragraphs of the oration, where Barlaeus addressed three types of public. The first of these are the rulers of the republic, whom he urged to help and protect the school: 'Defend, indeed advance, not as much those whom you have invited here with great rewards as the humanities, without which no republic ever was or ever will be ornate and well provided.' Barlaeus again illustrated the hierarchy he envisioned between trade and wisdom: the city government should reward the latter, not the former. To bring home his point, he added that they should invite Minerva, goddess of erudition, humanity and wisdom into the city: not to teach the citizens to trade, but to be wise.[110] Barlaeus' words to Amsterdam's rulers contained not just a plea for support, but also a coveted warning. Minerva, after all, also teaches 'by what counsels [kingdoms and cities] rise and fall'.[111] The message is clear: for now, the city government had chosen to spend its money wisely, namely on the Athenaeum Illustre. Should they change course, they would encounter the ephemeral value of their riches.

The second group of people Barlaeus addressed were the merchants, whom he called 'most noble, respected and learned men'. He asked them, whether citizens or immigrants, to be kind to the school in mind and in speech. They would find a place of solace and quietude in the school, where they would learn to value literature and its teachers, and realize the world of knowledge was much larger, and brought more enduring rewards, than the

109 Secretan, Le 'Marchand Philosophe' 13.
110 Barlaeus, The Wise Merchant 119, 4-20.
111 Ibidem 119, 14.

physical world they were so keen to explore.[112] Although Barlaeus' choice of words was kind, his message was again crystal clear: philosophy was much more useful than trade, and the merchants would do best to remember it.

Finally, Barlaeus addressed the city's youth. Barlaeus only spoke briefly to them, but addressed them most kindly as 'this republic's hope'.[113] By studying Plato and Aristotle, they 'will not only liberate [their] intellect from the filthy mould of ignorance, but also triumph over [their] enemies: anger, pleasure, desire, audacity, ambition, prodigality'. Barlaeus had high hopes for their advancement, and clearly desired them to become the third type of merchant Pythagoras envisioned: the type that only observes the marketplace, rather than participates in it. He, therefore, spurred them to value learning over riches: 'Do not believe that your life is what you draw from the air, but that it is what you draw from your studies; do not think it splendid to have the shine of gold or silver around you, but to shine with the light of learning.'[114]

In the true spirit of the humanist educators, Barlaeus put his faith in the youngest generation, which would benefit most from the teachings of the Athenaeum Illustre. While the older generations might be flattered into thinking they were *mercatores sapientes*, this generation might still learn the true value of learning, and choose it over trade altogether. In this manner, Barlaeus proved himself to be the wisest among the merchants: he had assured himself of the older generation's support, thus allowing him to educate their sons towards a different future.

Anna-Luna Post

112 Ibidem 123-125.
113 Ibidem 123, 15.
114 Ibidem 123, 24-28.

CASPARIS BARLÆI

MERCATOR SAPIENS,

SIVE

ORATIO

De conjungendis

Mercaturæ & Philofophiæ

ftudiis:

HABITA

In Inaugurationem Illuftris Amftelodamenfium Scholæ,

V. ID. IAN. CIƆ IƆ C XXXII.

AMSTERDAMI,

Ex Typographia GVILIELMI BLAEV,

CIƆ IƆ C XXXII.

Title page *Mercator Sapiens*, Amsterdam: Blaeu, 1632

Principles of this edition and translation

Editions and collated copies

Willem Blaeu, a well-known Amsterdam publisher, made a hand-some folio edition of the *Mercator sapiens* in 1632. After that, the oration was published in *Casparis Barlaei orationum liber,* a collection of Barlaeus' orations published by Willem's heir, Johan Blaeu (three editions: 1643, 1652, 1661). I have collated two copies of the first edition: the Gallica online copy[1] and the copy kept in the Leiden University Library.[2] I have found only one stop-press correction, which is in the headers. The text as such is identical throughout both copies.

The second edition, in the 1643 *Orationum liber,* follows the first one punctiliously, preserving accents, spelling and punctuation with very few exceptions. I have collated one copy[3] to find out whether Barlaeus himself made any changes to the second edition, and it seems that he did: he added an 'A.O.' ('Auditores Ornatissimi') at the beginning and had the Erasmus quotation (p. 100) printed in italics to make it even clearer that those were not his own words – he'd had enough trouble with orthodoxy as it was.

Since the editions by Sape van der Woude (1967, reprint AUP 2012, available online) and Catherine Secretan (2002) are not critical, I have ignored them; Van der Woude in fact introduced quite a few errors into the text.

---

1   Bibliothèque nationale de France, département Littérature et art, X-803 (1).
2   UBL 186 A15:6.
3   Staatliche Bibliothek Regensburg, 999/Ling. 455, made available online by the Bayerische Staatsbibliothek.

Presentation of the Latin text

The present edition stays close to the original in several of its aspects. For various reasons, I have chosen to maintain spelling (including the use of V for U and j for consonant i), accents, punctuation and use of capitals. It makes no sense to try and force a seventeenth-century text into the system of 'Classical' Latin that was in fact invented in the nineteenth century. In Barlaeus' time, consistency was not a goal in itself. Not even experts of Latin thought it undesirable to have the spellings *pretiosus* and *preciosus* in one sentence, as they occur in the *Mercator sapiens* (p. 120, 17f.). The accents – which Barlaeus uses sparingly – are a practical help to readers now as then, distinguishing e.g. the adverb *quàm* from the pronoun *quam*. Early modern punctuation, on the other hand, can be a challenge to readers who are unfamiliar with its principles. Modern punctuation systems are syntactical in nature, while seventeenth-century punctuation is rhetorical and indicates shorter and longer breath pauses. Thus the long breath pause that we call a full stop can occur within a period (in which case it is not followed by a capital letter), and a comma indicating a short breath pause can be placed where it is illogical in the syntactical system. Reading a sentence out loud will always help and moreover gives an insight into how Barlaeus himself delivered his oration on 9 January 1632.

Some typographical characteristics of the original edition, on the other hand – such as the use of ligatures and tildes –, are too impractical to preserve and would rarely be useful to the reader. Most paragraph separations have been introduced by me, in part following Van der Woude's edition. I have silently corrected a few apparent typographical errors, and have not resolved abbreviations that were the norm at the time (D. for *Dominus*, for instance).

Style and translation

The *Mercator sapiens* can be seen as one long *captatio benevolentiae* – the traditional beginning of an oration where the speaker tries to capture the audience's favour – not just for Amsterdam's new Illustrious School but for Barlaeus himself, who was relatively new to the city and who had faced difficult times over his Remonstrant inclination. The oration's style is highly polished, every sentence carefully constructed, every turn and phrasing chosen with deliberation. But the freshly appointed professor made sure that his literate style and show of erudition never resulted in an impenetrable fortress of syntactical difficulties.

It is hard to imagine for us, but since we know that the new academy in fact aimed to have the city's merchants among its students and lectures were solely given in Latin, we must assume that a reasonable part of Barlaeus' audience could understand at least the gist of what he was saying. Latin was then what English is now, *mutatis mutandis*. By the same token, seventeenth-century Latin was usually very practical and was influenced by the various vernaculars. Barlaeus' style in the *Mercator sapiens* is no more than an ornate version of the everyday Latin that was written by scholars everywhere; his periods may be long, but they are never nearly as complicated as Cicero's.

In translating this oration I have stayed as close to the original as possible while creating a readable English text. I have aimed for a credible translation that avoids anachronisms and conveys the dignified character of Barlaeus' oration. I have consulted the translations by Secretan and Van der Woude incidentally, but checked my entire translation against the seventeenth-century Dutch translation by Wilhelmus Buyserius, teacher at the Latin School of Enkhuizen.[4]

Corinna Vermeulen

4   Casparis Barlaei *Verstandighe Coopman, of Oratie, handelende van de t'samenvoeginghe des Koophandels, ende der Philosophie*, printed for the translator, Enkhuizen 1641.

Caspar Barlaeus

Mercator sapiens

TEXT AND TRANSLATION

CASPARIS BARLAEI

MERCATOR SAPIENS,

SIVE

ORATIO

5   De conjungendis

Mercaturae & Philosophiae

studiis:

HABITA

in inaugurationem Illustris Amstelodamensium Scholae,

10   V. ID. IAN. MDCXXXII.

1-10   Casparis Barlaei Mercator Sapiens sive Oratio de conjungendis Sapientiae et
Mercaturae studiis, in Illustris Amstelodamensium Gymnasii Inaugurationem. *1643*

Caspar Barlaeus

The Wise Merchant

Oration on Combining the Pursuit of Trade and Philosophy,
Held to Inaugurate the Illustrious School of Amsterdam
on 9 January 1632

Magnificis, Amplissimis, Prudentissimis,
Doctissimisque V.V. ac D.D.
IANO GROTENHVYS,
Praetori,
5   IACOBO DE GRAEF,
THEODORO BAS,
ANTONIO OETGENS,
ANDREAE BICKER,
Augustissimae Amstelodamensium Reip. Coss.
10   Nec non ejusdem Reip.
SCABINIS, SENATORIBVS,
ac Ill. Scholae CVRATORIBVS,
De re litteraria, Illustri Schola, ac me
praeclare meritis,
15   ORATIONEM
hanc Inauguralem,
Ex officio D. D. D.
CASPAR BARLAEUS.

1–18   1643 does not have the dedication; the prayer is printed after the oration,
followed by the date it was delivered.

To the generous, honourable, prudent and learned gentlemen
Jan Grootenhuys, sheriff,
Jacob de Graef, Theodoor Bas, Antoni Oetgens, Andries Bicker,
burgomasters of the august Republic of Amsterdam,
and this republic's eschevins, councillors, and board members
of the Illustrious School,
who have deserved highly of literature, the Illustrious School
and myself,
this inaugural oration is dutifully devoted and dedicated by
Caspar Barlaeus.

Precatio ad Deum opt. max. praemissa Orationi.

Omnipotens, aeterne Deus, pater Domini nostri Iesu Christi, rogamus Te supplices, ut hunc diem, quo Illustris hujus Scholae natalem celebramus, S.P.Q.A. faustum, felicem ac salutarem esse velis. Stat coram Te supplex Respublica, et grande coeptum tuis auspiciis inchoat. Stat supplex Ecclesia, et cum sine te nihil possit, tanti operis incrementa à te solo poscit. Stat supplex civium ordo, et charissima sua pignora, clementiae tuae in terris deposita, in novo hoc Musarum sacrario ad virtutis et sapientiae aram gloriae tuae ac cultui devovet. Stat supplex Iuventus, et seminarii hujus futura seges studiorum suorum fructus nomini itidem tuo ac patriae saluti consecrat.

Da, clementissime Deus, ut civitas haec pomeriis amplissima, civibus frequentissima, commerciorum fama celebris, amplioris famae precium ex doctrinae precio reportet. Fac eam res divinas scire, quae humanas amat impensius. Fac eam res humanas scire, quam post divinas humana quoque scire interest. Fac divina scire, ut divina imitetur. Fac humana scire, ut divina praéferat. Petat à Philosophia animi medicinam, quae à lucro corpori delitias quaerit. Petat à Philosophia curarum solatia, quae in mercimoniis invenit sollicitudinum plena omnia. Tum vere opulentam se credat, non cum fluxae felicitatis praesidia ostentabit, sed sapientiae ac eruditionis immobili peculio gloriabitur.

Tu Deus per Sapientiam urbem hanc constituisti: tot diversarum gentium homines per eandem in vitae societatem convocasti, domiciliis, conjugiis ac linguae communione conjunxisti. Da,

Prayer to God Almighty, spoken before the oration

Almighty, eternal God, Father of our Lord Jesus Christ, we humbly
beseech you to make this day on which we celebrate the birth
of this Illustrious School a fortunate, happy and beneficial day
for the senate and people of Amsterdam. Before you stands the   5
supplicant republic to commence a great undertaking under your
auspices. Before you stands the supplicant church, and since it
cannot accomplish anything without you, it looks to you alone for
the growth of this great work. Before you stands the supplicant
citizenry to dedicate its beloved children – pledges of your mercy,   10
deposited on earth – to your glory and worship at the altar of
Virtue and Wisdom in this new sanctuary of the Muses. Before
you stands the supplicant youth, and the future harvest of this
seminary consecrates the fruits of its studies both to your name
and the prosperity of the fatherland.   15

Grant us, most merciful God, that this city, so ample in territory,
so busy with citizens, so renowned for its commerce, gain greater
renown from the value of its learning. Make it know godly things,
as it loves human things all too much. Make it know human
things, as after the godly things it is also in its interest to know   20
the human. Make it know the godly so that it may imitate the
godly. Make it know the human so that it may prefer the godly.
Let it seek the mind's medicine from philosophy, as it looks for
the body's pleasure from lucre. Let it seek solace from sorrows in
philosophy as it finds worries everywhere in merchandise. May   25
it believe itself to be truly rich, not as it shows off the defences
of fleeting happiness, but as it glories in the enduring property
of wisdom and learning.

You, Lord, have founded this city by wisdom;[1] by wisdom you
have gathered people from many nationalities to share their   30
lives, you have brought them together in households, marriages,

1   Variation on Proverbs 3:19.

ut ejusdem Sapientiae beneficio arctius coëat Reip. hujus com-
pages, cives sapiant magis, vivant sanctius, pecuniae, gloriae et
voluptatum amorem recta ratione moderentur, ut quibus totus
mundus possessio est, discant vel hoc unum, paucissimis egere
Sapientem. Haec prima sit eorum Sapientia, ut Te cognoscant
verum Deum, et quem misisti Iesum Christum. Haec altera sit
eorum Sapientia, ut cum opes peregrè, domi virtutes indagent,
et unum hoc à se alienum putent, quicquid à virtute alienum
fuerit. Haec summa eorum sit Sapientia, ut operum tuorum in
hoc Naturae theatro magnitudinem, varietatem, pulcritudinem
contemplentur, et in iisdem bonitatis tuae, sapientiae, potentiae
manifesta documenta suspiciant et venerentur.

Amplissimos hujus Reip. rectores, Praetorem, Consules, Scabinos,
Senatores, Curatores, intelligentiae, et prudentiae Spiritu instrue,
ut concreditam sibi navem inter tot fluctus et Symphlegadas,
quibus res humanae jactantur, in publicae salutis portum
dirigant. Pastoribus Ecclesiarum, quotquot in hac urbe Christi
nomen ex verbi tui praescripto profitentur, gratiam tuam largire,
ut quod suadent piè, persuadeant potenter; quod docent sanctè,
credatur religiosè; quae monent salubriter, praestentur salutariter.
Divulsa Ecclesiae tuae membra collige, ut quos distraxit opini-
onum diversitas, uniat potentior charitas. Civium animos amore
mutuo colliga, et dissidiorum omnium causas longè ab hisce
moenibus abesse jube.

and a shared language. Grant that by the benefit of that same
wisdom the structure of this republic may grow together more
closely, that its citizens may be wiser, may live more saintly, may
moderate their love of money, glory and pleasures with sound
reason – so that those to whom the entire world is property,   5
may at least learn this one thing: that a wise man needs very
little. Let this be their first wisdom: that they know you as the
true God, and know Jesus Christ whom you have sent.[2] Let this
be their second wisdom: that while they pursue riches abroad,
they seek virtues at home, and that they consider alien to them   10
only whatever is alien to virtue. Let this be their highest wisdom:
that in this theatre of nature they contemplate the magnitude,
the variety, the beauty of your works, and in them respect and
revere the manifest proofs of your goodness, wisdom and power.

As for the honourable rulers of this republic – the sheriff, the   15
burgomasters, the eschevins, the councillors, the board members [of the Illustrious School] –, provide them with the spirit
of intelligence and prudence so that amid the many waves and
Symplegades[3] by which human matters are tossed, they may steer
the ship entrusted to them into the port of public prosperity.   20
As for all the church ministers who by the precept of your word
profess Christ's name in this city, grant them your grace, so that
what they piously preach may powerfully persuade; that their
holy teachings may be religiously believed; that their salubrious
admonitions may be followed salutarily. Gather together the   25
members of your church that were torn apart, so that those
who were separated by diversity of opinions may be united by a
prevailing love.[4] Bind the citizens in mutual love and banish all
causes of dispute from these city walls.

2   Combination of John 6:29 and John 14:1.
3   Greek mythology: a pair of clashing rocks at the Bosporus, pulverizing anything
that tried to pass between them.
4   1 Corinthians 12 and 13.

Da, ut Mercuriales hactenus, jam Sapientiae candidati audiant; parci, sed cum elegantia; pecuniae studiosi, sed sine detrimento melioris studii, hoc est, artium et virtutis. Scholae hujus primordiis benedic, ne doctrinae solum aut inanis scientiae, sed et probitatis magistra et mater audiat. Adauge dona tua in nobis, ut dum juventutem erudire muneris nostri est, eam feliciter erudiisse gratiae tuae imputemus. Adolescentium animos optimarum artium cupidine accende. Quibus pudor est nescire, discant tua opera. quibus pudor est peccare, in lege tua ambulent, et se pietate Tibi, obsequio parentibus, docilitate praeceptoribus probent; ne desint aliquando, qui Remp. hanc prudentibus consiliis fulciant, Ecclesiam facundis vocibus doceant, Scholas denique salubribus praeceptis regant. Audi, exaudi nos per et propter filium tuum Vnigenitum Iesum Christum, qui tecum et Spiritu sancto vivit et regnat in aeternum verus Deus, Amen.

Let those who were thus far known as followers of Mercury[5] now be called candidates of Wisdom; frugal, but with elegance; eager for money, but without detriment to a better pursuit, that is: the pursuit of the arts and of virtue. Bless the beginnings of this school, so that it may be called not just a teacher and mother of learning or useless science, but also of probity. Augment your gifts in us, so that while it is our duty to educate the young, we may attribute it to your grace that we have successfully done so. Set the adolescents' minds ablaze with a desire for the greatest arts. Let those who are ashamed of their ignorance learn your works;[6] let those who are ashamed to sin walk in your law[7] and prove themselves with piety to you, with obedience to their parents, with docility to their teachers; so that there will be no lack one day of those who may prop up this republic with prudent counsel, teach the church with eloquent voices, and lead the schools with beneficial teachings. Hear us, hearken to us, through and because of your only Son, Jesus Christ, who lives and rules forever as true God with you and the Holy Spirit. Amen.

5   Roman god of trade, eloquence, communication, travellers, trickery and thieves.
6   Psalm 90:16.
7   2 Kings 10:31, 2 Chronicles 6:16.

ORATIO
In Illustris Amstelodamensium Scholae Inaugurationem.

Amplissime D. Praetor, Magnifici spectatissimique Consules et
5   Scabini, Senatores gravissimi, Syndici prudentissimi, Curatores
dignissimi, Pastores Ecclesiarum vigilantissimi, Doctores,
Magistri, et Scholarum Rectores doctissimi, Cives, Mercatores
humanissimi, Iuvenes studiosissimi, et quotquot frequentes ad
hanc Panegyrin confluxistis:

10 Quoties urbem hanc vestram, jam quoque meam, intueor, et oculos per ejusdem decora omnia et ornamenta circumfero; pendeo
animi, quid primum in ea, quid secundum, quid postremum
mirari debeam. Hic me sacra Deo templa, tot afflictae paupertatis
augusta receptacula, turres et minantes in coelum Phari: illic
15 injecta fluminibus repagula et cataractae; alibi mercantium
augustae porticus, tot ubique pontium fornices et laquearia
spectantem tenent. Est, ubi mercium peregrè advectarum
stupendam vim, ubi navium multitudinem ac robur, ubi portus
capacissimos, ubi circumfusas urbi classium stationes attonitus
20 adspectem. Amplitudinem ejus si oculis metiri velim, avocat me
aedificiorum splendor. cum in splendore haereo, interturbat
civium frequentia. cum hanc attentius considero, in tanta multitudine, Rectorum prudentiam, legum reverentiam, subditorum
obsequia, modestiam, et quod caput rei est, ordinem suspicio.

25 Nec illud leve puto, in eam me civitatem translatum cerni, quae
stagnis paludibusque undique innatat, ubi tantorum operum
molem portant ligna, librant silvae, et florentissimum totius
Europae emporium suffulciunt putrescentes pini. Vt prorsus
in ejus magnitudine constituenda natura et labor, virtus et
30 fortuna, tellus Oceanusque contendisse videantur. Quae quidem
omnia, quanquam eximia, sumtuosa, admiranda sint, famamque

10   intueor, A.O. et *1643*

Caspar Barlaeus
Oration to inaugurate the Illustrious School of Amsterdam

Honourable Lord Sheriff, generous and respected burgomasters
and eschevins, most worthy councillors, wise guild representa-
tives, magnificent curators, reverend ministers of the churches,   5
most learned doctors, teachers and school directors, respected
citizens and merchants, studious youngsters, and you all who
have come in great numbers to hear this panegyric!

Every time I look upon this city of yours – which is now my city
as well – and let my gaze wander over all its marvellous sights,   10
I deliberate as to what I should admire in it first, what second
and what last. Here the churches sacred to God hold my gaze, so
many lofty homes for the afflicted poor, towers, lighthouses rising
up to the sky; there, the dams and sluices built in the streams;
elsewhere, the lofty porticoes of the traders; everywhere, so many   15
bridges' arches and ceilings. There are places where I can look in
astonishment at the tremendous amount of goods shipped in from
abroad, the multitude and strength of the ships, the capacious
ports, the landing stages for fleets that surround the city. If I
want to measure its wide extent with my eyes, I am distracted   20
by the splendour of its buildings; as I consider the splendour,
the crowd of citizens presses in between; as I look at the crowd
more attentively, in such a multitude I admire the prudence
of the regents, the observance of the law, the obedience of the
subjects, their modesty, and the main thing: their orderliness.   25

Nor do I think lightly of the fact that I have been transferred to
this city that floats on pools and swamps everywhere, where the
weight of such great buildings is borne by wood and balanced by
forests, where the most flourishing trade centre of all Europe is
supported by rotting pines. Nature and labour, virtue and fortune,   30
earth and sea seem to have vied with each other to make this
city great. All of this, however, although it is excellent, splendid

opulentissimae urbis domi forisque differant: minora tamen putanda sunt isto Amplissimi Senatus Consulumque instituto, quo nova ac insolita huic loco ratione, à Sapientiae et literarum studiis, earumque publica professione, novum Reipublicae suae decus hoc die affectare incipiunt.

Vtique placuit Viris gravissimis ac prudentissimis, ut quae Mercurii hactenus fuit sedes, ac Pluti domicilium, jam Palladis quoque ac Phoebi sacrarium audiat; opum splendorem doctrinae radiis illustret, divitiasque tum demum rectè aestimare discat, cum earum usum è Philosophorum monumentis hauserit. Et profectò conveniens erat, urbem illam, quae opum fama orbem universum replet, tandem de immortalitatis praesidiis cogitare. conveniens erat, cives mercimoniis intentos filios in spem majorem educare, ut quas fluxas possident opes, optimarum artium scientia et nominis perennitate solentur, quarum illa vivis eripi nequit, haec ne mortuis quidem potest. Nec illustrius quicquam ac gloriosius, quam eos ipsos populos, quos emundi vendundique amor ex omni terrarum parte huc excire solet, ad literarum quoque mercatum proficisci, nec tabernas solum et merclum promtuaria, verum Musarum etiam penetralia frequentare, et aures à forensi strepitu fessas suavissimo earum alloquio recreare. Atque hujus quidem laudatissimae rei cum initium faciat praesens hic dies, ex prisco Scholarum more quaedam praefabor, et Minervam, illam Sapientiae Deam, inter arma ac Martis strepitus, inter libertatis

and admirable, spreading at home and abroad the fame of a most prosperous city, should be considered less important than this project of the honourable council and burgomasters, by which on this day they begin to pursue a new jewel in their republic's crown in a manner that is new and unusual to this place: from the study of wisdom and literature, and public classes on these subjects.

Certainly these earnest and prudent gentlemen have decided that the city that so far was Mercury's home and Plutus'[8] residence should now also be called the shrine of Athena[9] and Apollo;[10] that it should shine the rays of learning on the splendour of its riches, and finally learn to estimate its wealth correctly once it will have grasped its use from the philosophers' teachings. And it was definitely appropriate for this city, renowned throughout the world, to finally start thinking about the fortresses of immortality; it was appropriate for the citizens, intent on merchandise, to start educating their sons toward a greater hope: that they may assuage the transience of the riches they possess with the knowledge of the arts and the perpetuity of their names – the former cannot be taken away during one's life and the latter not even after death. Nor is there anything more magnificent and glorious than the fact that the very peoples drawn here from every part of the earth by the love of buying and selling will now also go to the market of literature and frequent not only the shops and warehouses but also the inner chambers of the Muses, resting their ears which are tired from the noise of the marketplace by listening to the Muses' sweet words. And since today marks the beginning of this praiseworthy undertaking, I will speak some introductory words after the old custom of the schools, and among armed conflict and the din of Mars,[11] among

8   Greek god of wealth. One of the less important gods in Greek religion.
9   Greek goddess of wisdom and war.
10   Greek and Roman god of music, truth, prophecy, medicine.
11   Roman god of war.

nostrae discrimina, et reciprocos bellorum aestus huic Reip.
aeternum consecrabo.

Quamobrem istiusmodi mihi argumentum delegi, quod loci
hujus ac civium genio, et opulentissimi Emporii studiis aptum
5   esse putavi; piscatores illos imitatus, qui hamo appendere solent
illicem ac lenocinantem escam. Equidem ita semper statui,
operosè illos ineptire, qui in foro Lapitharum pugnas recitant,
in castris Dialecticum torquent enthymema, in sacris regnorum
imperiorumque momenta exaggerant, in mensis super Hecubae
10   aut Andromaches fato singultiunt, in Scholis iis exercitationibus
fatigant adolescentulos, de quibus ad Senatum referri expediat:
Ideoque praeter rem me facturum putavi, si apud mercatores,
apud lucri avidam gentem, inter pecuniarum tinnitus, in urbe
quaestui dedita, de aliis rebus, quam de mercatura, lucro, opi-
15   busque disseruero: non ut eos mercari doceam, sed sapienter; non
ut lucrandi artes praescribam, quas ingenue fateor me ignorare,
sed ut optimas vobiscum probem; non ut opum studia damnem,
sed rectae rationis sufflamine coërceam. Illud ostendam: Op-
timum esse Mercaturae cum Sapientiae ac litterarum studiis
20   commercium, nec augendae rei curam mentis contemplationibus,
nec has illi obesse, verum optimis rationibus inter se conspirare,
mercandi et philosophandi facultatem, ut tanto mihi felicior
sit futurus mercator, quanto philosophari poterit luculentius.
Audivere de rebus suis disserentes Philosophos Athenae,

the dangers to our liberty and the alternating tides of war,[12] will consecrate Minerva,[13] goddess of wisdom, to this republic forever.

For this reason I have chosen a subject that in my opinion suited the character of this city and its citizens as well as the interests of a very wealthy trade centre – imitating fishermen who attach a decoy to the hook, an enticing bait. I have always said that it is a complete waste of effort to sing of the Lapiths'[14] battles in the marketplace, to spin out a dialectical argument in an army camp, to exaggerate the importance of kingdoms and empires in church, to bemoan the fate of Hecuba[15] or Andromache[16] at the dinner table, and at school to wear out adolescent boys with exercises better brought before the senate. Therefore I decided that for an audience of merchants, a people hungry for profit, to the clinking of money, in a city devoted to financial gain, it would be beside the point for me to talk of anything but commerce, profit, and wealth. Not to tell them how to trade, but to do it wisely; not to teach them the arts of making a profit – which I can honestly say I do not know – but to examine, together with you, which are the best; not to condemn the pursuit of wealth, but to keep it in check with the brake of reason. This I will show: that trade and the pursuit of wisdom and the arts go together very well, and that neither the care for augmenting one's wealth is in the way of the mind's contemplations, nor vice versa. On the contrary, the human faculty for trade and that for philosophy work together in the best of ways: the more brightly a merchant can philosophize, the luckier I will deem him. Athens listened to philosophers

---

12   Barlaeus here refers to the battle of Slaak on 12 September 1631, in which the fleet of Holland and Zeeland defeated the Spanish. Barlaeus composed a laudatory poem for this occasion.
13   Roman pendant of Athena.
14   A legendary Greek tribe famous for its battle against the Centaurs.
15   Wife of Priam, ruler of Troy, sold into slavery after the Greeks conquered Troy.
16   Wife of Priam's son Hector, who was killed by Achilles in the Trojan War. Her son Astyanax was thrown off the city walls by Neoptolemus, who then made her his concubine.

legislatores Lacedaemon, censores Roma. Nec grave erit, opinor, Amstelodamensium populo, si de mercatorum excellentia, virtutibus et officio disserentem audiat, minorum licet gentium, Peripateticum. Quod dum ago, A[uditores] O[rnatissimi], animum
5 mihi ab hac ipsa, de qua loquar, pecuniarum curâ paulisper vacuum commodate.

Vetus admodum res est mercari. sed et sapere. ut nesciam, an à Sapientia profectam esse mercaturam, an ab hac Sapientiam fluxisse, statuere debeam. Illud certum, mutuam semper ope-
10 ram haec studia praestitisse, cum sine mercium permutatione humanis necessitatibus consuli non posse sapientes crediderint, et per eandem rursus magnis incrementis ad prudentiam iri in confesso sit. Quippe erectius mercantibus ingenium est, et dum dolo circumveniri impensè cavent, sapientiam in consilium
15 advocant. Acuit curas lucri spes, spem utilitas. utilitatem commendat indigentia, quae per varios usus exercitatissima artem fecit non uno modo rem faciendi. Hinc arbitror à veteribus emundis vendundisque mercimoniis praefici, non iracundum Martem, non lascivientem Venerem, non socordem Lunam, non
20 ridiculum Vulcanum: sed ingeniosissimum Deorum Mercurium, illum sapientiae ac eloquentiae autorem. Nempe ut doceant, et sapientia et facundia opus esse mercantibus; illâ, ut quaestum honestum à turpi discernere possint; hac, ut verborum lenocinio commendent eas merces, quas extrudere satagunt. Quam ob
25 causam eidem gallum affingunt, vigilantiae symbolum; ut doceant matutinum esse debere mercatorem et vigilem, in omnes occasiones intentum, ut rem faciat.

25   Gallum *1632 1643*

talking about its business, Sparta to legislators, Rome to censors. Nor will it be troublesome for the people of Amsterdam, I think, if they hear an Aristotelian talking about the excellence, virtues and duty of merchants, albeit of lesser peoples. And as I do so, my friends, please let me have your attention for a while, free from the very care for money of which I will speak.

Trade is an ancient thing, but so is wisdom – so I do not know whether I should say that trade was born from wisdom, or the other way around. This much is certain: these two pursuits have always benefited one another, as the wise have always believed that it was impossible to solve human problems without exchanging merchandise, and on the other hand it is well known that through such an exchange, big steps are made towards prudence. For traders have sharp minds and while they do their best to prevent being duped, they take counsel with wisdom. The hope of gain sharpens the attention, usefulness sharpens that hope. Usefulness is commended by need, which, highly practised through various experiences, has invented the art of doing something in more ways than one. Hence, I think, the ancients have appointed to oversee the buying and selling of goods, not ill-tempered Mars, not lascivious Venus,[17] not languid Luna,[18] not ridiculous Vulcan,[19] but Mercury, cleverest of the gods, creator of wisdom and eloquence. They did so in order to make it clear that merchants need both wisdom and a way with words – the former to be able to distinguish an honest profit from a disgraceful one, the latter to recommend with enticing words the goods they are busy selling. For this reason, they link him to the rooster, symbol of vigilance, to make it clear that a merchant should be a watchful early riser, intent on any occasion to do business.

17 Roman goddess of love.
18 Personification of the moon in Roman mythology.
19 Roman god of fire, volcanoes and metalworking.

Dudum est, quod in Sticho exclamaverit Plautus: Quàm benè re gesta salvus convertor domum, Neptuno grates habeo et tempestatibus, simul Mercurio, qui me in mercimoniis juvit, lucrisque quadruplicavit rem meam. Antiquitatem certè et primos mercaturae natales non aliunde rectius, quam ex lite-rarum monumentis ac sapientum libris investiges. Docent illi, primis seculis, cum naturae opibus census omnes constarent, intrà pecora agrosque illam constitisse, primosque mercatores agricolas et pastores fuisse. Docent illi, decantatam illam in Scholis Philosophorum justitiae commutativae appellationem, à negotiatoribus profectam, ut jam ipsius Philosophiae moralis partem conficiat, haec ipsa, de qua loquor, facultas.

Aristoteles in iis libris, quibus politicum format, de mercatoribus praecepta tradit; ut ostendat, ad sapientis etiam perfectionem facere, has artes nosse. Et divinus ille Plato, ubi de constituendâ Republicâ laborat, mercatores in eam adscisci vult, non eos solum, qui res corporeas precio emunt et vendunt: sed et illos, qui animi cultum, scientias, artesque honesta mercede aliis divendunt. Quin et Platone antiquior Pythagoras, totum mercatum in tria hominum genera distinxit, quorum alii prodiissent ut venderent, alii ut emerent, quod utrumque genus dicebat sollicitum esse, ac proinde minus felix: alios non ob aliud venire in forum, quam ut spectatores agant, quos ille solos felices esse perhibebat, quod vacui curis gratuita voluptate fruerentur.

It's long ago that Plautus[20] exclaimed in his *Stichus*: 'Inasmuch as, my business prosperously carried on, I am returned safe home, thanks do I return to Neptune[21] and to his tempests; to Mercury as well, who in my traffic has aided me, and by my profits has rendered my property fourfold.'[22] Certainly the antiquity of trade and its origins are best investigated on the basis of the teachings of literature and the books of the wise. They tell us that in the beginning, when all riches consisted in the resources of nature, trade was an exchange between herds of cattle and arable land, and the first traders were farmers and herdsmen. They tell us that the appeal to justice of exchange, often repeated in the schools of philosophers, stems from tradesmen – so the very faculty of which I speak already provides part of moral philosophy.

Aristotle in the books in which he shapes the politician hands down lessons on merchants in order to show that knowing these arts is relevant to the perfection of a wise man as well. And where the divine Plato concerns himself with creating a republic, he wants merchants to be included in it; not only those who buy and sell material things at a price, but also those who sell to others the cultivation of the mind, the sciences and the arts for an honest fee.[23] Even Pythagoras, who came before Plato, distinguished the entire marketplace into three types of people: those who had come to sell, those who had come to buy – both these types, he said, are agitated and consequently less fortunate – and the third type, who come to the market merely to watch, the only type he named fortunate, because without worries they enjoy a free pleasure.[24]

---

20 Roman playwright, *c.*254–194 BC.
21 Roman god of the seas.
22 Plautus, *Stichus* III.i, 402–405 (transl. Riley).
23 Plato, *Republic* II.
24 A variation is in Diogenes Laertius, *Lives of Eminent Philosophers* VIII, 1:8. In this variation, the third type is compared to the philosopher, who seeks truth rather than fame or gain and thus has nothing to sell or buy.

Homerus, quo homine Graecorum nemo plura novit, nemo, quae
ad usum faciunt, copiosius docuit, tantum mercaturae precium
esse credidit, ut ipsam Pallada sapientiae Deam, quasi alio habitu
non posset, mercatoris induerit. Vbi enim Telemachum alloqui-
tur, et se Mentem fingit, suaviter ait Pallas, se maria sulcare, ut
ferrum, quod navibus vehebat, aere Temesino permutaret. En
mercantem Pallada. Quin et ipse Panomphaeus Iupiter, è cujus
cerebro ortam fingunt Pallada, in celebri illa apud Lucianum
vitarum auctione, universam Philosophorum turbam, vili satis
pretio, distraxit. En mercatorem Iovem.

Illud amplius constat, primam mercaturam, humanitatem et
sapientiam, una cum mercibus per universum orbem circum-
duxisse. Solon, qui Athenis leges condidit, et plerique Graecorum
illo commercio suas res tulerunt ad exteros, ac vicissim fecere, ut
exotica sui cives viderent. Plutarchus cum vitam sapientissimi
hujus Solonis enarrat, eo, inquit, tempore mercatura gloriosa erat,
cujus opera cum Barbaris consuetudo, cum Regibus amicitiae
contrahebantur. Quare tanto Spartanos, sapientem alioquin
populum, à vera Sapientia longius abfuisse arbitror, quanto
iniquiores mercantibus lucra prohibuerunt. De Gallis scribit
disertissimus Caesar, eos Mercurium maximè coluisse, utpote
artium omnium inventorem, viarum atque itinerum ducem,
quem ad quaestum pecuniae, mercaturasque vim maximam
habere arbitrabantur. Et quam familiare fuerit Romanis, sapien-
tissimo alioquin populo, pecunias locare, aes alienum contrahere,
versuris faciendis luculenti patrimonii naufragium facere, docet
erudita illa Satyrâ Flaccus, in qua sub persona Mercurialis

Homer, the most knowledgeable of all the Greeks, who taught the most generously what is relevant to practice, valued trade so highly that he gave Pallas Athena herself, goddess of wisdom, the appearance of a merchant, as if he could have chosen nothing else. For when she addresses Telemachus, pretending to be Mentes, Pallas sweetly says that she sails the sea to exchange the iron she transports on her ships for copper from Temesus.[25] So Pallas Athena is a merchant. Even Jupiter Panomphaeus, of whom the story is told that Pallas was born from his brain, in Lucian's famous auction of lives sells off the entire crowd of philosophers at a bargain price.[26] So Jupiter is a tradesman.

This furthermore is clear: that the first trade brought not only merchandise, but humanity and wisdom throughout the world. Solon,[27] who established the laws at Athens, and many Greeks took their own things abroad in such an exchange, and vice versa effected that their own citizens got to see exotic things. Plutarch in his story of the life of this most wise Solon says that in those days trade was full of glory, because through it familiarity with Barbarians and friendships with kings were established.[28] For this reason I deem the Spartans, a wise people in other respects, the further from true wisdom the more unjust they were in forbidding merchants to make a profit. The eloquent Caesar writes of the Gauls that they greatly revered Mercury as the inventor of all the arts, the guide of roads and routes, whom they considered to have the greatest power for acquiring money and for trade.[29] And how normal it was for the Romans (otherwise a most wise people) to lend money, to run into debt, to wreck a splendid family fortune by borrowing money to pay their debts, Horace tells us in the learned *Satire* in which, in the person of the merchant

25 Homer, *Odyssey* 1.105, 1.78, 1.420.
26 Lucian, *Philosophies for Sale* (LCL 54).
27 Athenian politician and poet (*fl. c.*600 BC).
28 Plutarch, *Life of Solon* 2.3, 2.4 (transl. Perrin).
29 Julius Caesar, *De bello gallico* VI, 17.

Damasippi illos sui seculi taxat negotiatores, qui postquam, ad
medium Ianum, rem fregissent, et magni instar Biantis Priene
sua nudi egrederentur, sero ad philosophiam se conferebant.
Ex quibus colligo, summos doctrinae ac Sapientiae proceres,
uti aliarum omnium artium, ita et mercaturae ac Philosophiae
commune vinculum agnovisse, et de his ipsis, quas tractamus
rebus, serio verba fecisse.

Sed propius libet mercantium virtutes expendere, et depromtis
è Philosophia gravibus praeceptis ostendere, quam et illorum
vitiis mederi possit Sapientia. Ac primum illud mercatorem at-
tendere monet Sapiens, ne nimium appetat. Id enim egit rerum
natura, ut ad benè vivendum non magno apparatu opus esset. Qui
immodicas opes sectantur, immodicis saepè excidunt, et dum
omnem felicitatis suae spem pelago ac ventis credunt, avaritiam
paupertate ac ignominia mulctant. atque ita dum alios sua
luxuria, alios ambitio praecipitat, hos inconsulta ac Prudentiae
monitis destituta lucri cupiditas. Nihil refert, quantum in aerariis
jaceat, si non quaesita, sed quaerenda semper computamus. Non
enim qui plus habet, sed qui minus cupit, dives est. nec pauper,
qui minus habet, sed qui nimis cupit. Infinitum est, quod petit,
qui plus petit, quam quod deest. Cleanthes philosophus rogatus,
qui dives evadere posset, cordatè respondit, si cupiditatum
fuerit inops. Alia atque alia desiderantibus, desunt haec ipsa,
et inter magna vota inopes sunt, qui dum Orientem pariter ac
Occidentem animo devorant, eam beatitudinem sibi fingunt,

Damasippus, he censures those tradesmen of his time who after
they had ruined their business on the marketplace and had to
leave town naked like the great Bias[30] left Priene, turned to
philosophy when it was too late.[31] From these stories I conclude
that the greatest men of learning and wisdom recognized a link   5
between trade and philosophy, as between all the other arts,
and spoke seriously of the very things we are now discussing.

But I would like to consider the virtues of merchants more closely
and demonstrate with some serious precepts borrowed from
philosophy how wisdom can also remedy their shortcomings.   10
The wise man first admonishcs the trader that he should take
care not to want too much. After all, the world is arranged so
that there is no need for great splendour to live well. Those who
are after immoderate wealth often suffer immoderate losses; as
they entrust all their hope of happiness to the sea and the winds,   15
they are punished for their greed with poverty and shame. Thus
while some are brought down by their extravagance, others by
their ambition, these men are brought down by an ill-considered
desire for financial gain that is without the precepts of prudence.
It does not matter how much we have in our coffers if we are   20
always calculating not what we have gained but what remains
to be gained. For not he who has more is rich, but he who desires
less. Nor is he poor who has less, but he who desires too much. If
one asks for more than what is lacking, there is no end to what one
asks. When the philosopher Cleanthes was asked how he could   25
become rich, he wisely answered that he could if he were destitute
of desires.[32] People who always want something else and then
something else again lack precisely these things; and those who,
devouring both the east and the west in their minds, imagine a
state of happiness that they will never attain, are destitute amid   30

---

30 One of the legendary 'seven wise men' of Greece; he lived in the city of Priene
in the sixth century BC.
31 Horace, *Satires* 2.3.
32 Stobaeus, *Florilegium*, ed. Meineke (1856) vol. III p. 196, 28.

quam assequuntur nunquam. Philosophus animum hominis
divitem appellat, non loculos. qui quantumvis pleni sint, dum-
modo pecuniae cupiditate laboret animus, pauper es. Divitiae
ex copia aestimari solent, at copiam non aliunde rectius, quam
5   ex rerum satietate colligas, quam quoniam non assequitur, qui
plura appetit, nunquam omninò futurus est dives.

Fingite alicui ex magno auri acervo vivendum sumtuosè, tectis
laqueatis, veste superba, famulis decem, supellectile ad invidiam
exquisita; alteri illa contemnenti ad sumtum sufficere sestertia
10 centum: uter dives censendus? ille qui vanae cupiditatis man-
cipium semper eget? an alter, qui contracto cupidine abundanti
similior est? Nec enim censum aestimatione, sed victu ac cultu
aestimandum sapientes prodiderunt. Nec plura possidet, qui
pluribus ad se suosque tuendum eget, quam qui paucissimis.
15 Mecum sentit mascula et severa Stoicorum schola, qui quotquot
coelo et terra frui datum, divites pronunciabant. nec quicquam
tam angusti et parvi esse animi, quam eas res minus amare non
posse, ad quas hominum vulgus inflammatum aviditate rapitur.
At Peripatetici, familiares nostri, quibus nihil est uberius, nihil
20 eruditius, nihil gravius, uti pecunias aliaque vitae hujus praesidia
minimè fastidiunt, ita eorum omnium amorem mediocritate
definiunt. nec immerito disputant, utrum expediat aliquem
plurium esse bonorum dominum, quam custos esse possit.

Illud praeterea mercatorem nostrum didicisse gaudet Philoso-
25 phus, quod cum opibus abundet, mores suos iisdem non tradat,
nec cum Craesos vicerit, Numa esse desinat. Caducum hoc omne

their great desires. A philosopher calls a man's mind rich, not his coffer. For no matter how full it is – as long as your mind suffers from desire for money, you are poor. Riches are estimated from abundance, but abundance will be concluded most correctly from a satiety of things – which is never attained by one who wants more and therefore he will never be rich, ever.

Imagine someone who has to live sumptuously from a big stack of gold, with panelled ceilings, magnificent dress, a staff of ten servants, with furniture so exquisite that he is envied; and another, who despises all that, and for whom a hundred sesterces are sufficient to cover his expenses. Which one should we consider rich? The man who, being a slave to vain desire, is always needy? Or the other man, who resembles one living in abundance more because he has curbed his desire? For the wise have revealed that wealth should be estimated not with a valuation, but by one's way of life and one's culture. Someone who needs many things to provide for himself and his family does not possess more than someone who needs very little. The masculine and strict school of the Stoics agrees with me: they proclaimed rich whoever could enjoy the sky and the earth, and claimed that nothing was so narrow-minded and silly as being unable to love those things less to which the masses are drawn, inflamed with greed. But the Aristotelians, our friends who are the summit of abundance, learning and earnest, although they certainly do not despise money or the other protections of this life, still limit the love of all that with moderation; and they rightly question whether it is convenient for someone to be the master of more goods than he could be the guardian of.

A philosopher moreover is glad that our merchant has learnt that while he abounds in riches, he should not deliver his character to them, and that while he has surpassed Croesus,[33] he should

33 Croesus (595–546 BC) was the last king of Lydia (the west of present-day Turkey), famous for his immense wealth.

et mobile esse ducit, quod possidet, nec tam virtutis atque ingenii,
quam fortunae ac temporum esse munera. Noverat hoc quoque
Lacon iste, qui cuidam Lampen Aeginetam efferenti, ac felicem
praedicanti, quod praedives videretur, nihil se morari, inquit,
5   felicitatem è funibus pendentem. Sapientia divitiis pro ratione,
non pro libidine uti monet. Sapientia minores animos gerere
vult, quotquot fortunae praejudicio majores habentur. Nec enim
vitiorum adminicula esse debent pecuniae, aut in Creatoris sui
dedecus, sed gloriam; neque in proximi perniciem, sed com-
10 moda ac salutem conferri. Sapientia opulentos non fastidit, sed
exosculatur unicè. illos nempe, qui locupletes sunt sine ullius
injuria, magnifici sine luxu, liberales sine ostentatione, graves
sine morositate, religiosi sine superstitione.

Erectae et bonae mentis mercator, (inter quales hic loquor, inter
15 quales hic vivo) sicut vitiosas merces à probis, ita virtutes a vitiis
distinguit, et quot domi numerat talenta, totidem virtutum officia
sibi praescribit. Cum nummos suos attentius intuetur, fingit
uni insculptam pietatem, alteri candorem, alteri fidem, alteri
prudentiam, alteri liberalitatem, et in ipsis malorum irritamentis
20 imagines honesti concipit. Vt cum totos pecuniarum acervos
seponit, totum quoque virtutum chorum seposuisse videatur.

not stop being Numa.[34] He considers all that he possesses to be
ephemeral and transient, and to be the gifts of good fortune and
the times rather than of virtue and cleverness. That was also well
known to the Spartan who, when someone extolled Lampis of
Aegina and called him fortunate because he seemed extremely   5
rich, told the man that he himself was not interested in good
fortune that hung from ropes.[35] Wisdom teaches us to use wealth
in accordance with reason, not wantonness. Wisdom wants all
those to behave modestly who are considered important by the
prejudice of fortune. For money should not be the support of bad   10
habits, nor should it be used to shame its Creator, but to His glory;
not to the detriment of one's neighbour, but to his comfort and
well-being. Wisdom does not despise the well-to-do, but approves
of them especially: of those, that is, who are affluent without
harming anyone, magnificent without decadence, generous   15
without ostentation, serious without being morose, religious
without superstition.

A merchant of upright and good character – like the people I am
talking to here, and am living amongst – distinguishes virtue
from vice as he distinguishes bad from good merchandise, and   20
as many talents[36] as he counts at home, so many virtuous duties
does he appoint himself. When he looks closely at his coins, he
imagines that piety is stamped onto one, honesty onto another,
faith onto another, onto another prudence, kindness onto yet
another, and in the very incentives to evil he imagines pictures   25
of what is honourable. So when he lays aside whole stacks of
money, it is as if he has laid aside a whole chorus of virtues as
well. Consequently, the more gold he possesses, the less he sins;
the more his gold shines, the humbler he likes to be; the more

34   Numa Pompilius, the legendary second king of Rome, was renowned for his
wisdom.
35   Plutarch, *Apophthegmata Laconica* 69 (*Moralia: Sayings of Spartans*) LCL
245: 410-411. Plutarch's anecdote mentions the fact that Lampis owned many ship
cargoes, which explains why his riches are 'hanging from ropes'.
36   Ancient measure used for precious metals.

Quo ergo copiosius aurum possidet, eò minus peccat: quo ful-
gidius aurum possidet, eò humilior esse amat: quanto lucratur
saepius, tanto in munifici Dei laudes reflectitur crebrius; quanto
lucratur rarius, tanto providentiae divinae causas suspicit religi-
5   osius. Quod si rationes turbaverit scriba, foro cesserit debitor, aut
preciosam mercium saburram sorpserit mare, facile à Philosophia
solatium petet, qui praeter virtutem reliqua minus aestimare
didicerit: qui vitae subsidia modo his, modo illis liberaliore
manu applicari, et iisdem pene, quibus mare, aestibus adfluere
10   et refluere attentius perpendet.

Quamobrem, qui, rebus nonnihil accisis, animum prorsus
despondent, Deos nescio quos increpant, jam in coelum, jam
in mare convitia jaculantur, sapientes non sunt. A Philosophis
quippe accipient: Nihil viro bono praestandum, praeter culpam:
15   Divitem sat esse, qui, cum vel omnia desint, sibi non deest: nec
desperandum illi, qui rerum omnium egenus omnia bona in
spe habet: Orbem singularium esse, et per vices possideri, hunc
bonorum ejus parte excuti, ut reponatur alteri. Nec dubium est,
quin major sit futura materies animum firmandi in paupertate,
20   quam divitiis, cum in hac summa vis virtutis sit, non inclinari,
nec deprimi. Quare divitias non minus absentes, quam praesentes
parvi faciet, quia nec advenientes eas sentiet immoderatius,
nec recedentes. Terras omnes suas putabit, etiam cum nullas
habebit, et quas habet, tanquam quae aliorum esse possunt,
25   non respuet, sed amabit segnius. Paradoxa vobis loqui videor.
Nec diffiteor. Verum haec Aristippi, haec Socratis sapientia fuit.
Ita Zeno, Cleanthes, Crates, Chrysippus, Epictetus sentire, ita
loqui amavere.

often he makes a profit, the more frequently he reflects on the praise of the generous God; the less often he makes a profit, the more religiously he respects the causes of divine providence. And if his clerk has messed up the books, if a debtor has gone bankrupt or the sea has taken a precious load of goods, he will easily seek solace from philosophy, since he has learnt to value anything else less highly than virtue, and closely considers that the comforts of life are given more generously now to the one, then to the other, and tend to come and go in tides much like those of the sea.

Therefore they are not wise men who completely lose heart when their business is in a bit of trouble, who rail against I don't know what gods, who swear at the sky and then at the sea. From the philosophers they will certainly hear that a good man need not answer for anything but guilt; that he is sufficiently rich who does not fail himself, even if everything fails him; and that he does not have to despair who, destitute of everything, has all the good things in his hope; that there is only one world and it is possessed taking turns, and one man is driven out of a share of its good things so that it may be given to another. And there can be no doubt that there is more opportunity to strengthen one's character in poverty than in wealth, because in poverty the greatest strength of virtue is not to yield and not to be depressed. For this reason he [the wise merchant] will consider absent riches as unimportant as present ones, because he will not feel too strongly about them whether they come or go. He will consider all the lands his own, even if he has none; the lands that he has he will not despise but love with more resignation, as if they may belong to others. You think I am talking paradoxes, and I do not deny it. But in fact this was the wisdom of Aristippus and of Socrates. This is what Zeno, Cleanthes, Crates, Chrysippus and Epictetus thought and how they liked to talk.[37]

37 Classical and Hellenistic philosophers, most of the Stoic school.

Etiam hoc in mercantibus laudabile et praedicandum quàm maximè, quod ingenti lucro aucti secum et cum Paupertate dividant, et ex aurea messe spicilegium aliquod egentibus indulgeant. Habet, non dicam Fortuna, sed benignior Deus, suas
5   rationes, et inter alias hanc quoque, ut quibus favit liberalius, alios pari liberalitate sublevent. Non decedit danti, quicquid accedit homini, et cum hominem esse commune sit diviti et pauperi, humanum quoque est, huic nihil deesse, sine quo homo esse non potest. Dedit Deus, ut quod dedit, per eos reciperet, quibus
10 minus dedit. Dedit, ut exemplo suo ad piam magnificentiam invitaret, qui sine exemplis boni esse nequeunt. Dedit, ut qui gratis dare nesciunt, praemium expectent ab eo, qui solus sine spe praemii dare potest.

Iam verò in Emptione et Venditione quanti est, nihil utile putare,
15 quod non simul honestum sit, nec privatis commodis postponere recti conscientiam. quantum est, etiam si fraus occultior sit, non fallere velle, vel sui damno in contractibus sincerum ac veracem esse. Ac de his summa relligione in Officiorum libris disputat Cicero, ac admirabilem virtutis speciem ob oculos ponens, ab omni
20 fuco alienas esse vult negotiationes, rigideque urget illas veteris aevi sanctissimas formulas: Inter bonos benè agier oportet: Omnia ex aequo et bono metienda; et fide bona. Quin eos conscientiae casus excutit, homo à veri Dei cognitione alienissimus, quos nos flocci-pendimus, et in contrahendo propius honestatis momenta

In merchants it is also praiseworthy and to be most highly commended that when they have made a huge profit they should
divide it between themselves and poverty, and from a golden
harvest should allow the needy to glean some ears. I will not
say Fortune, but rather God, who is more merciful, has His own   5
reckonings, and among them this one: that those whom He
has favoured generously should support others with the same
generosity. Whatever accrues to a man is not lost to the one who
gave it, and since the rich man and the pauper have in common
that they are human, it is also human that the pauper should   10
lack nothing without which one cannot be human. God gave in
order to receive back what He gave through those to whom He
gave less. He gave in order to invite to pious generosity by His
example those who cannot be good men without an example. He
gave so that those who cannot give without expecting anything   15
in return might expect their reward from Him, who alone can
give without hope of a reward.

Now in buying and selling, how important it is to think nothing useful unless it is honourable as well, and not to let one's
conscience come after one's personal benefit. How important it is,   20
even if the deceit would be hard to detect, not to want to deceive,
and to be sincere and truthful to one's own loss when closing a
deal. Cicero discusses this with the utmost conscientiousness in
his *De officiis* (*On Duties*): placing an admirable image of virtue
before our eyes, he wants all business to be free of deceit, and   25
strictly insists on those sacred formulas of ancient times: Between
good men, dealings should be fair; All things should be measured
by what is right and honest, and in good faith. He even examines
– he, a man completely alien to the knowledge of the true God –
those cases of conscience that we consider trivial, and examined   30
the moments of honesty while entering into a contract more
closely than we do, who are proud to call ourselves Christians.[38]

38   Cicero, *De officiis* III 1.

expendit, quàm qui illustri Christianorum titulo gloriamur. Nihil
illi, nihil Panaetio ac Antipatro, priscis Philosophis, utile visum,
quod non simul honestum esset, nihil honestum, quod non etiam
utile. quae quanquam philosophantium cogitatione distrahi
possint, in vita tamen communi perniciosissimè divelluntur.
Si enim ad virtutem, aut virtutis actionem nati sumus, omnino
sequitur, illud ipsum, quod honestum est, summum bonum
esse, et cum summi boni ratio nullum in se bonum desiderari
patiatur, etiam utile in se includat necesse est. Accedit, quod,
cum utilitas res secundum naturam sit, vitium omne naturae
hominis et rectae rationi adversum; nec inhonestum cum utili,
neque honestum cum inutili stare queant.

Et profectò nulla exitialior opinio in vitam hominum irrepsit,
quam quae honestum ab utili distraxit. Vnde enim malae fidei
contractus, falsi testes, illicita fenora, versurae, aeruscandi artes,
monetae arrosiones, nisi quod dum mercamur, emolumenta in
mercibus intuemur, at quod in iis improbum, quod injustum,
quod fallax, non videmus. Ille in Philosophia nostra multum
se profecisse sciat mercator, qui si vel homines injuriam celare
possit, aut proposita immunitate injustus, facinorosus, veterator,
malitiosus esse, nullius tamen compendii spe à virtute recedit.
Sed libet ex veterum sententia rigidius mercari.

Like the ancient philosophers Panaetius[39] and Antipater,[40] he deemed nothing useful that was not honourable at the same time, and nothing honourable that was not useful as well.[41] In philosophical thought the two can be separated, but in everyday life it is disastrous to detach them. For if we are born to virtue or to acting virtuously, it certainly follows that precisely that which is honourable is the highest good; and since the nature of the highest good precludes that anything good be lacking in it, it necessarily includes the useful. Moreover, because usefulness is in accordance with [human] nature, while all vice is contrary to man's nature and sound reason, the dishonourable cannot coexist with the useful, nor the honourable with the useless.[42]

Indeed no view more destructive has ever crept into men's life than that which separates the honourable from the useful. For where do contracts in bad faith, false witnesses, illegal interest, loans to pay debts, sleight-of-hand tricks and shaving off coins come from, if not from the fact that when we trade, we look at the profit in the commodities and do not see what is dishonest, unfair, or deceitful in them? That merchant should know that he has advanced far in our philosophy who, even if he could hide an injustice from people or be unjust, criminal, malicious or a con man with impunity, nonetheless does not stray from virtue for the sake of profit. No, we want to do business more strictly, in accordance with the view of the ancients.

---

39 Panaetius of Rhodes (185–110 BC) was a Stoic philosopher whose works have not survived. His *On Duties*, however, served as a source for Cicero's work of the same name.

40 Antipater of Tarsus (d.129/130 BC) was Panaetius' teacher and is discussed by Cicero as well.

41 Cicero, *De officiis* III 11.

42 *De officiis* III 11.

Iudicat idem Cicero, injuste improbeque illum facturum, qui,
ut pluris vendat, quicquam eorum, quae ipse noverit, emtorem
celabit. Marci Catonis sententia fuit: Qui in venundando vitium
scisset, et non pronunciasset, emtori damnum praestare oportere.
5 Volunt ergo, ut exemplo rem illustremus, aedes vitiosas, male
materiatas, ruinosas, vel pestis contagio afflatas, ignorantibus
haec ipsa locari aut vendi non debere. Loquar clarius: Si è Galliis
vir bonus in hanc urbem magnum frumenti numerum advexerit,
idque in summa annonae caritate, si idem sciat plures mercatores
10 è Galliis solvisse navibus frumento onustis, quaerunt Sapientes,
dicturusne id sit civibus Amstelodamensibus, an silentio
suum quam plurimo venditurus! Negabit dicturum Diogenes
Babylonius, magnus alioquin et gravis Stoicus, cum qui silet
suum vendat, sine insidiis agat, nulli injuriam faciat, quia jure
15 civili illud dicere non constringitur. Affirmabit contra Cicero,
cum Antipatro philosopho acutissimo, celandum hoc non esse,
cum ea lege natus sis, ne publicae saluti officias, et ut homo de
hominibus, civis de concivi benè merearis. Quod si illos improbat
Cicero, qui reticent dicenda, quid sentire eundem aestimatis de
20 iis, qui in vendendo orationis adhibent vanitatem? Equidem,
cum hominis, ad summi Dei imaginem conditi, majestatem nihil

The same Cicero judges that he who hides something he knows from the buyer in order to get a better price acts unjustly and dishonourably.[43] Marcus Cato's[44] opinion was as follows: if the seller knew of a defect and kept silent about it, he should compensate the buyer for his loss.[45] So to illustrate the matter with an example, they hold that houses that are defectuous, badly constructed, decaying or contaminated with a disease should not be rented or sold to parties who are ignorant of this.[46] Let me speak more plainly: if an honest man from France has shipped a large quantity of grain to this city at a time when the price of grain is very high, and he knows that several other merchants have set sail from France with ships full of grain, the wise ask whether he should tell the citizens of Amsterdam this, or sell his grain at the highest possible price by keeping silent. Diogenes of Babylon,[47] otherwise a great and worthy Stoic, will say he shouldn't tell them, since the reticent merchant sells his own goods, acts without deceit and does no one injustice, because he is not obligated by civil law to tell.[48] Cicero on the other hand, with the very sharp-witted philosopher Antipater, will state that the information should not be concealed, because you are born under the law that you should not obstruct public welfare and as a human being should do well by other human beings, and as a citizen by fellow-citizens.[49] Now if Cicero disapproves of those who conceal what should be said, how do you think he judges those who tell lies when selling?[50] To be sure, since nothing befits the greatness of man, who was created in God's

5

10

15

20

25

---

43 *De officiis* III 50.
44 Marcus Porcius Cato 'the Censor', Roman statesman and writer (234–149 BC).
45 *De officiis* III 66.
46 *De officiis* III 55.
47 Also known as Diogenes of Seleucia (*c.*230–*c.*150 BC); pupil of Chrysippus and teacher of Panaetius.
48 *De officiis* III 51, 52.
49 *De officiis* III 52.
50 *De officiis* III 58.

magis deceat, quam veracitas, nec simulabit, nec dissimulabit
vir bonus quicquam, vel ut emat melius, vel ut vendat. Ethnici
hominis oraculum est: Non licitatorem venditor, nec qui contrà
licitatur, emtor apponet: uterque si ad eloquendum venerit, non
5   plus, quam semel, eloquetur.

Intelligitis, opinor, non vobis solum, sed etiam priscis Quiritibus
placuisse sinceritatem, simplicitatem, candorem; displicuisse
astus et fraudes. Et quanquam constet, haec ipsa vulgo minus
turpia haberi; ideoque nec legibus, nec jure civili prohiberi; tamen
10   mecum creditis, naturae lege sancitum esse, nihil insidiosè,
nihil simulatè, nihil fallaciter agendum. Quàm verò illa sunt
apud Ciceronem subtiliter et ad admirationem honesta, cum
negat, Sapienti fas esse, in naufragio homini tabulam eripere,
cui semel adhaesit: cum adulterinos nummos, quos imprudens
15   accepit, negat sapientem, cum id rescierit, soluturum pro bonis:
cum ei, qui aurum vendit, putans esse orichalcum, indicare
vult virum bonum, aurum illud esse, ne denario emat, quod
sit mille denariûm: cum promissa servanda esse negat, quae
non sunt iis utilia, quibus promisimus. Breviter, cum omnium
20   mercantium et in vita civili honestè versantium, unam hanc vult
esse regulam, ut aut illud, quod utile videtur, inhonestum non
sit: aut si inhonestum est, ne videatur esse utile.

image,[51] more than veracity, a good man will neither simulate nor dissimulate anything to make a better purchase or sale. A pagan's verdict is: The seller shall not bring in a bidder, nor the buyer a counter-bidder; when it comes to naming a price, neither shall name a price more than once.[52]   5

I think you understand that it is not just you, but also the ancient Romans who like sincerity, simplicity, candour, and who dislike cunning and deceit. And although it is a known fact that the latter commonly are not considered all that shameful, and are therefore not prohibited by any regulations or civil law, you will   10
agree with me nonetheless that natural law has laid down that nothing should be done insidiously, dishonestly or deceitfully. How subtly and admirably honest are the passages in Cicero where he says that a wise man in a shipwreck may not wrest the plank from a man who has gotten hold of it; [53] where he states that   15
a wise man who has unwittingly accepted forged coins, once he has realized they are forged will not pay a debt with them as if they were genuine;[54] where he says that if someone is selling gold while he thinks it mere fool's gold, a good man should point out to him that it is gold, so that he will not buy for a *denarius* what   20
is worth a thousand;[55] when he tells us that promises should not be kept if they are not useful to those to whom we made them. In short: when he says that all those who conduct trade and are honourably engaged in public life should have this one rule, that either that which they think useful should not be dishonourable,   25
or if it is, they should not think it useful.

---

51 Genesis 1:27.
52 *De officiis* III 61.
53 *De officiis* III 89.
54 *De officiis* III 91.
55 *De officiis* III 92.

Erasmus Roterodamus, immortale Bataviae nostrae decus, ad hanc Ciceronis hominis Ethnici in contractibus sanctimoniam, usque adeo stupet, ut parùm absit, quin inter coelites et beatorum animas Ciceronem locet. In Praefatione siquidem in Tusculanas quaestiones, in haec verba prorumpit: Quid aliis accidat, nescio. me legentem sic afficere solet M. Tullius, praesertim ubi de benè vivendo disserit, ut dubitare non possim, quin illud pectus, unde ista prodierunt, aliqua divinitas occuparit. Atque hoc quidem meum judicium mihi magis blanditur, quoties animo reputo, quàm immensa sit, quàmque inaestimabilis aeterni numinis benignitas, quam quidam ex ingenio suo nimis in angustum contrahere conantur. Vbi nunc sit anima Ciceronis (verba Erasmi sunt) fortasse non est humani judicii pronunciare. Me certè (Erasmi verba loquor, non mea) non admodum adversum habituri sunt in ferendis calculis, qui sperant illum apud Superos beatam vitam agere. Haec Erasmus. Non ego.

Verum relicto Cicerone, et qui Ciceronem penè apotheosi donavit, Erasmo, pergam Sapientiae monitis mercatorem componere. Ab hac audiet: Non esse temere spondendum, cum noxa praesto sit: fidendum esse, sed videndum cui: non omnia emenda esse, ne necesse sit mox cum Castore omnia vendere: cavendas esse fenerationes in perniciem publicae societatis comparatas. Monet eadem, cauti uti simus in nominibus et syngraphis faciendis. Quamvis enim in tabulis addas mille cautiones, et juris laqueos, quibus debitor constrictus teneatur, omnia tamen eludet versutissimus Damasippus. Fiet aper, modo avis, modo saxum et, cum volet, arbor, et in jus vocatus alienis maxillis ridebit.

Erasmus of Rotterdam, immortal ornament of our Holland, is so astonished by the pagan Cicero's scrupulousness regarding contracts that he is not far from giving him a place among the inhabitants of heaven and the souls of the blessed. For in his preface to the *Tusculanae quaestiones*, he bursts out: 'I don't 5 know what happens to others, but Cicero always affects me in such a way – particularly when he speaks of living well – that I cannot doubt that the breast from which those words came was possessed by some divinity. And I like this view of mine even more when I consider how immense and how unfathomable God's 10 goodness is, although some try to confine it to a narrowness based on their own minds. Where Cicero's soul is now' (these are still Erasmus' words) 'may not be for human judgement to say. I for one' (still Erasmus' words, not mine) 'shall not disagree all that much in the vote with those who hope that he leads a blessed 15 life in heaven.'[56] This is what Erasmus says, not I.

But leaving behind Cicero, and the man who practically gave him an apotheosis, Erasmus, I will proceed to compose the merchant from the admonitions of wisdom. From wisdom he will hear that one should not make rash promises because harm is near; that one 20 should place trust, but take care in whom; that one should not buy everything, lest one must soon sell everything like Castor;[57] that one should be careful of usury that is set up to the detriment of public society. Wisdom also warns us to take care when drawing up bonds or contracts. For although you add a thousand securities 25 and legal snares to bind the debtor, the cunning Damasippus will elude everything. He will change his shape to a boar, then to a bird, then to a rock, and to a tree when he wants, and when summoned to court he will laugh with another's jaws.[58]

---

56   Desiderius Erasmus, *M.T. Ciceronis Quaestiones Tusculanae* (Basel 1523) fol. 3r, available online (http://reader.digitale-sammlungen.de/resolve/display/bsb11217457.html).
57   Martial, *Epigrammata* VII 98.
58   Horace, *Satires* II 3.

Et cujus quaeso est disputare? Vtrum magnatibus et nobilibus sit permissum mercari; Philosophi. utrum liceat ex pecuniis usuram petere; Philosophi. utrum fas sit carius quicquam vendere, quam emisti; Philosophi. Quis de tota mercatura praecepta
5 tradit, quis sordidam ab opulenta, tenuem à copiosa distinguit? quis depromtis ex jure naturali, gentium, civili praeceptis eam universam ordinat? Politicus est. At hunc universae Philosophiae principem et architectona vocat Aristoteles. Quis mercantibus non minus, quam Iurisconsultis, sua principia largitur, Honestè
10 esse vivendum, alterum non laedendum, suum cuique tribuendum: Ethicus est. Quis docet, in commutationibus vel rerum cum rebus, vel rerum cum pecuniis, vel pecuniae cum pecuniis rei familiaris habendam esse rationem? quis familias exhaurire, nomina facere, rem fidemque consumere vetat? Oeconomicus est.

15 Aristoteles, quo viro nemo philosophatus est sanius, Prudentiae civilis administras comitesque facit, Experientiam, Memoriam, Solertiam, Ingenium, Sententiam et Consilium. At hae ipsissimae sunt mercaturae partes et officia. Experientia quando et quatenus et ubi mercandum docet. Memoria debiti creditique rationes in
20 numerato habet. Ingenium de rebus mercibusque rectè judicat. Solertia ea media excogitat lucrandi, quae à versutia, et pravis artibus absunt. Consilium mercaturam universam moderatur et regit. Sententia prudentiorum facta et judicia in commutandis mercibus respicere monet, ne, dum soli sapere nobis videmur,
25 fortunae naufragium debeamus. Audivistis ergo, quam se cum morali Philosopho maritet mercatura. Paucula ex Speculativa Philosophia petamus, ne hanc quoque se fastidire dicat operosus negotiator.

And I ask you, whose job is it to discuss whether great men and nobles are allowed to trade? The philosopher's. Whether it is permissible to charge interest on money? The philosopher's. Whether it is right to sell something at a higher price than you have bought it? The philosopher's. Who gives rules for the entire trade, who distinguishes filthy from respectable trade, poor from abundant? Who brings order to the entire trade with rules taken from natural, international and civil law? The politician. Now he, according to Aristotle, is the prince and architect of the whole of philosophy.[59] And who presents the merchants as well as the lawyers with his principles: that one should live honourably, should not harm another, should give everyone what he is entitled to? The moral philosopher. Who teaches us that in an exchange of things for things, of things for money, or of money for money, one should take into account the family's interests? Who forbids us to empty out the family, to make debts, to squander our property and credibility? The household economist.

Aristotle, whose philosophy is the soundest of all, calls these the assistants and companions of civil prudence: experience, memory, shrewdness, intelligence, judgement, and counsel.[60] Now these very things are the parts and duties of trade. Experience teaches us when, to what degree, and where we should trade. Memory has the calculation of our debts and credits at hand. Intelligence gives a correct judgement of circumstances and goods. Shrewdness comes up with the means to make a profit while staying away from cunning and nasty tricks. Counsel oversees and rules the whole of commerce. Judgement warns us that we should heed the actions and opinions of more prudent men in exchanging goods, lest we shipwreck ourselves while thinking that we alone are wise. So you have heard how trade goes hand in hand with moral philosophy. Let us take a few things from speculative philosophy, lest the industrious businessman say that he despises that as well.

---

59 Aristotle, *Nicomachean Ethics* 1152b 2.
60 Aristotle, *On Virtues and Vices* 1250a 30ff.

Proprium mercantium est, commutare sedes, et facili mobilitate
per omnes terrarum plagas diffundere insatiabilem animum:
ire, quo fertilis alicujus orae, et in majus laudatae fama evocat.
Nihil tam immansuetum hospitio, horridum situ, coeli natura
5   intemperatum, quod non aliqua lucri spe patria abducat. At
horum omnium locorum situs, vias, maris vada, promontoria,
portus, quatenus cavendi, quatenus subeundi, nosse oportet.
Quae quidem omnia ex Geographia nostra peti possunt. Qui
verò singularum regionum sint proventus, commoda, messes,
10   ex physicorum quoque monumentis et rerum naturalium scriptoribus habemus. Docent hi Indiam ebur, Sabaeos thura, Persas
sericum, Moluccanos aromata, aurum argentumque Americanos,
Chalybes ferrum, aes Suecos, stannum Britannos sufficere.

Cumque expediat, ea ipsa, quae emit aut precio aestimat, nosse
15   ementem, de rerum naturis, metallis, arboribus, plantis, aroma-
tibus, animalibus, piscibus, avibus disserentes audiat Physicos,
Aristotelem, Theophrastum, Oppianum, Dioscoridem, Plinium et
polyhistora Solinum. Quaesita per mare Scythicum in Orientem
via unde, nisi ex his ipsis scriptoribus non subobscure colligi-
20   tur! Vnus Plinii locus tantae rei auspicium, licet inauspicatum

It is typical for merchants to change their residence, easily moving and allowing their insatiable spirit to roam all the earth's
regions – to go where the rumour of some fertile coast that is
praised all too highly calls them. No place can be so inhospitable,
so terribly located, so intemperate in climate, or it will lure them   5
away from home with some hope of profit. Now for all these
places one should know the location, the routes by land and sea,
the promontories, the ports, in how far one should steer clear
of them, in how far one should approach them – all of that can
be learnt from geography. But what every region's produce is,   10
its opportunities, its harvests, that we find in the works of the
natural philosophers and the writers on the world of nature.
They tell us that India supplies ivory, the Arabians incense, the
Persians silk, the Moluccans spices, the Americans gold and
silver, the Chalybes[61] iron, the Swedes copper, the Britons tin.   15

And since it is useful for the buyer to know what he is buying or
valuing, he should hear what the natural philosophers, Aristotle,
Theophrastus, Oppian, Dioscorides, Pliny and the learned Solinus
have to say on the natural world, metals, trees, plants, spices,
animals, fish and birds.[62] Where does one gather clear informa-   20
tion concerning the route to the East that is sought over the
Black Sea, if not from these writers? A single passage in Pliny
gave us a sign, although unexpected thus far, for a thing of such

61   A tribe from Graeco-Roman times, living on the south coast of the Black Sea
and known for selling iron.
62   Theophrastus (*c*.372–*c*.287 BC) was a philosopher and natural scientist.
His surviving publications include several extensive works on botany: Michael
Gargarin (ed.), *Oxford Encyclopedia of Classical Greece and Rome* (Oxford 2010),
s.v. 'Theophrastus', accessed 3 August 2017. The Graeco-Roman poet Oppian (2nd
century AD) published poems on fishing and birds, idem, s.v. 'Poetry, Greek'.
Dioscorides (1st century AD) travelled extensively and wrote several books on
plants and drugs, John Roberts (ed.), *The Oxford Dictionary of the Classical World*
(Oxford 2007), s.v. 'Dioscorides'. Gaius Plinius Secundus or Pliny the Elder (AD
23/4–79) is most famous for his encyclopaedic *Naturalis historia*. Gaius Iulius
Solinus (3rd century AD) wrote the *Collectanea rerum memorabilium*, a compilation
of historical and geographical curiosities.

hactenus, fecit, tanto facinori ansam dedit. Vnde didicimus Africam, etiam versus Austrum, superato Bonae spei promontorio circumnavigari posse, et hinc in Arabiam, Aegyptum, Persas iri, nisi ex eodem Plinio et Strabone! Quid Columbo, Vespucioque, primis Americae detectoribus, fiduciam fecit, ut relicto veteri orbe, novo exemplo, proras Occidenti obverterent? Aristotelis, Platonis, et fortè etiam Senecae loca in causa fuere.

Praeterea, ab Astrologis discet mercator, quae anni tempestivitates quibus locis adeundis, aut cavendis conveniant: ex coelo non dierum solummodo incrementa et decrementa, sed et horarum in mari momenta deprehendet: ex Cynosyrâ, quàm Septentrioni, quàm oppositae plagae vicinior: ubi et quantum deflectat ab Arcto acus magnetica, et quibus regulis naturae error corrigi possit. Et cum absque ventis, mari, aestu navigare negatum illi sit, utile fuerit, proprios regionum singularum ac partium maris ventos novisse. ut: Notum Adriatici maris arbitrum esse, Boream Germanici, Gallici Circium, Calabriae littorum Iapyga, Atabulum Apuliae, Athenarum Sciron paulùm ab Argeste deflexum, de quibus in Meteorologicis disputat Aristoteles. utile fuerit novisse, quae maria et quando procellosa, quae scopulis infesta, quae magis, quae minus, quae citius, quae tardius, quae nunquam

importance, and gave us a handle on such a great deed.[63] Where
have we learnt that one can sail around Africa to the south as
well by rounding the Cape of Good Hope, and from there reach
Arabia, Egypt and Persia, if not from the same Pliny and Strabo?
What gave Columbus and Vespucci, the discoverers of America,   5
the confidence to leave the Old World and point their prows
west, setting a new example? Passages in Aristotle, Plato, and
possibly Seneca[64] as well.

From the astronomers, moreover, the merchant will learn which
seasons are convenient for visiting which places, or avoiding them;   10
from the sky he will understand not only the lengthening and
shortening of the days, but also calculate hours and minutes at
sea; from the Little Bear, how much he is closer to the north than
to its opposite; where and how much his compass deviates from
the North Pole, and with what rules nature's error can be cor-   15
rected. And since he cannot possibly sail without the winds, the
sea and the tides, it will be useful for him to know the particular
winds of the separate regions and parts of the sea, for instance:
that the south wind is the arbiter of the Adriatic, the north wind
of the Baltic, the Circius[65] of the Gallic Sea,[66] the Iapyx[67] of the   20
Calabrian coasts, the sirocco of Apulia, the Sciron,[68] deflected
a little by the Argestes,[69] of Athens. Aristotle in his *Meteorology*
discusses them.[70] It will be useful for him to know which seas are
stormy and when; which are rock-infested; which have stronger
tides, which lesser, which have faster tides, which slower, and   25

63 Pliny the Elder, *Naturalis historia* VI 53.
64 Lucius Annaeus Seneca (*c.*3 BC–AD 65), Roman Stoic philosopher and writer.
65 The name of a violent west-north-west wind blowing in Gallia Narbonensis
(the south of France).
66 The stretch of sea between Sardinia and the Balearic Islands.
67 A wind that blows in southern Italy (which was also known as Iapygia).
68 A north-west wind blowing from the Scironic Rocks on the isthmus of Corinth
(which would make it a west wind, hence the mention of the Argestes deflecting it).
69 A north-west wind.
70 Aristotle in *Met.* 363b 25 does mention the Sciron and the Argestes, but most
of the information here comes from other sources.

aestuent, quam periculosa praetervectio promontorii australis Africae, quàm ex portu Sinarum in Iaponiam difficilis trajectus, quam infestae navigantibus maris Balthici fauces, quantus in sinu Mexicano à continente aquarum refluxus.

5 Illud quoque apud Philosophos reperire est, Oceanum perpetuo motu in occasum ferri, ideoque citius hinc Novum orbem adiri, quam illinc Veterem repeti. Est et ille motus in Scholis nostris decantatus, quo à Septentrione in Austrum mare movetur, qui in mari mediterraneo cernitur, ubi Maeotis per Bosphorum Cim-
10 merium in Pontum Euxinum fluit, Euxinus per Bosphorum Thracium in Propontidem, Propontis per Hellespontum in Aegaeum. Vt nihil dicam, de motu peculiari, qui in mari Adriatico ad oram Dalmatiae, Istriae, Illyridis, usque ad ultimos Venetorum recessus deprehenditur; ubi flexus in Meridiem maris impetus versus
15 Flaminiam, postea nonnihil ad Orientem se torquet; planè ut in orbem, ex littorum, uti opinio est, appulsu, circumagi videatur. At ille maris fluxus et refluxus quotidianus, uti inter naturae miracula est, ita solum philosophum disserentem patitur.

Amplius, non ignorare quempiam vestrûm opinor, quam ex usu
20 fiet vago mercatori, variis linguis loqui posse, et ad singularum gentium mores, vitaeque instituta se componere. Ergò si Graecos adire volet, Cecropis ore ipsi loquendum: si Venetos, Hetruscos, Ligures, Hispanos, Gallos, Latinas voces addidicisse conducet.

which have none at all; how dangerous it is to round the southern cape of Africa, how difficult to cross to Japan from the port of the Chinese, how hostile to sailors the mouth of the Baltic, how strong in the Gulf of Mexico the ebb from the continent.

In the philosophers one can also find that the ocean is carried toward the west in a perpetual motion, and that therefore sailing from here to the New World goes faster than from there to the Old. In our schools we also teach the motion by which the sea moves from north to south, which is seen in the Mediterranean, where the Sea of Azov flows into the Black Sea through the Cimmerian Bosporus,[71] the Black Sea into the Propontis[72] through the Thracian Bosporus,[73] and the Propontis into the Aegean Sea through the Hellespont. To say nothing of the particular movement which is seen in the Adriatic at the coast of Dalmatia, Istria and Illyria, all the way up to the deepest recesses at Venice, where the sea's movement is deflected south towards Flaminia[74] and then turns somewhat to the east, so that it appears to move in a circle, which is caused by its hitting the coast, it is thought. But the daily ebb and flow of the sea, as it is among nature's wonders, can only be discussed by a philosopher.

Furthermore, I think all of you know how useful it is for the wandering merchant to speak several languages, and to be able to adapt to the customs and way of life of the various peoples. So if he wishes to visit the Greeks, he will have to speak the language of Cecrops;[75] if he wants to visit the Venetians, the Etruscans, the Ligurians, the Spanish, the French, it will be profitable for him to have learnt Latin. Should he desire to traverse Arabia, Persia, Syria, Media, India, and practically all of the East, it is of

71 The Kerch Strait.
72 The Sea of Marmara.
73 Now simply called the Bosporus.
74 A district on Italy's Adriatic coast.
75 The mythical king of Attica who built the Acropolis.

Si Arabas, Persas, Syros, Medos, Indos, totumque ferè Orientem lustrare animus erit, Arabum quam maximè sermonem sciri interest. Quae omnia ex Scholis et ipsis Latinorum, Graecorum, Arabum libris addisci in confesso est. Nec vivere profectò apud exteros potest mercator, nisi qui gentium se ritibus, moribusque accommodare noverit. Quamobrem consulendi erunt scriptores clarissimi, qui in Aegypto à fabis abstinendum esse doceant: in Arabia cum bacillo ambulandum; in Persia non accumbendum, nisi unctis: in Germania hospitum officiis adblandiendum: Graecos rerum novarum esse avidissimos: Hispanos graves et inquieto ingenio: Italos injuriarum tenaces: Gallos civiles blandosque: Anglos Ioviales: Poenos perfidos: infideles Allobroges. quae peregrinum mercatorem nescire, et pudori saepe fuerit et dispendio.

Sed satis ostendisse mihi videor, quanta philosophantium et mercantium sit cognatio et societas, quamque ingens literarum et humaniorum artium in facienda mercatura momentum, cui tantum splendoris, dignitatis, ac precii ab illis ipsis artibus accedit, quantum aeterna caducis, animi bona terrestribus purgamentis potiora habentur. Restat, ut iis respondeam, qui, ut laudatissima coepta sugillent, clamitant: Nihil Mercurio cum Pallade commune esse: strepitus istos forenses aversari Musas, fugere turbulentam urbem, et secessus suos amare ac soliloquia: hic de augendo solum peculio cogitari, nec patientes aures animi culturae commodari. Quasi verò doctorum sermonibus magnas urbes

the greatest use to speak Arabic. It is well known that all these can be learnt in the schools and from the books of the Latin, Greek and Arab writers themselves. And the merchant certainly cannot live abroad unless he knows how to adapt to the ways and customs of other nations. He will therefore have to consult the   5 famous writers who tell us that in Egypt one should not eat beans; that in Arabia one should walk with a stick; in Persia one should not go to table unless anointed; in Germany one should praise the host's services; the Greeks are quite keen on novelties; the Spanish are serious and restless of mind; the Italians never forget   10 an offence; the French are courteous and friendly; the English jovial; the Carthaginians[76] are deceitful; the Allobroges[77] cannot be trusted. Ignorance of all this will often cause the merchant abroad embarrassment as well as financial loss.

But I think I have demonstrated sufficiently how close the affinity   15 and partnership is between philosophers and merchants, and how enormous the importance of literature and the humanities in conducting trade, which gains as much splendour, dignity and value from precisely these arts as the eternal is valued over the ephemeral, and the riches of the mind over the dirt of the earth.   20 Now I only have to respond still to those who try to revile this praiseworthy effort by crying that Mercury and Pallas Athena have nothing in common, that the Muses shun the noise of the market, flee the crowded city, and love their quiet places and soliloquies; that people only have thought for increasing   25 their private property here, and do not lend a patient ear to the cultivation of the mind. As if it were forbidden to hinder great cities with the words of learned men, or as if it were only permitted to listen to jokes or small-talk there. For the moment I will

76   Like several other peoples and tribes from Antiquity that Barlaeus mentions, the Carthaginians of course had long disappeared in his time; he no doubt means the inhabitants of northern Africa.
77   A Gallic tribe living in the region between what is now Lyon and Geneva; Buyserius in 1641 simply translates with 'Savoyards'.

illigari nefas sit, aut ludicros solummodo in iis sermones audiri
oporteat, aut rerum colloquia leviorum. Quibus in-praesentiarum
hoc respondebo, perperam illos philosophari, qui doctrinae
studia arceri volunt ab Emporiis, ob hoc, quod negotiorum plena
5   sint. cum non ob aliam causam iis locus hic esse debeat, quam
ut aures à mercantium strepitu fessae parumper requiescant,
et immoderatior pecuniarum cura praeclarissimarum rerum
meditatione castigetur. Quid, quod rectius in negotiis omnibus
versari possit, qui erudito Musarum otio rectè uti noverit. Quin,
10   et hoc contendo, cum ad opes eximias atque illustres accesserit
litterarum lumen, tum illud divinum quid ac singulare existere.

Sed pleni sunt omnes libri, plena exemplorum vetustas, quibus ita
statuisse illis temporibus sapientissimos viros constat; opulentis-
simas quasque urbes scholis, doctoribus, bibliothecis, aliisque
15   sapientiae instrumentis carere non posse. Athenae, Achaiae
metropolis, non mercantum solummodo concursu copioso, sed
et eruditissimis hominibus, liberalissimisque studiis affluens
fuit. Tarentum, Rhegium, Neapolis, plane non opum solummodo, sed et Graecarum artium, ac disciplinarum promtuaria
20   fuere. Capua, Antiochia, non tam civium frequentia, classium
robore, mercimoniisque inclaruere, quam iis artibus, quibus
aetas puerilis ad humanitatem informari solet. Massiliam quoque
Narbonensis Galliae maritimam urbem, linguarum artiumque
studiis olim viguisse ex Strabone et Tacito constat. Quin illa
25   terrarum gentiumque Dea Roma, annon simul et de expugnando
orbe et barbarie cogitare potuit? simul et exercitum ordinare,
et dicendi leges scribere? simul et Dictatorem castris praeficere,
et Oratores pro rostris loquentes audire? ut male profecto mihi

tell them this: that they philosophize incorrectly who want the pursuit of learning to be kept away from trade centres because the latter are full of business; for there should be a place for that pursuit here for no other reason than that the ears, tired from the merchants' noise, may rest for a while and the care for money 5 that is too immoderate may be chastised by the consideration of the greatest things. Indeed, the man who knows how to use the learned quiet of the Muses is able to handle himself better in any business. I will also assert that once the light of literature shines on exquisite and illustrious riches, a certain divine and 10 singular quality arises.

But all books and all Antiquity are full of examples from which we know that the wisest men already said as much in those times; that precisely the wealthiest cities cannot do without schools, teachers, libraries and the other instruments of wisdom. Athens, 15 the metropolis of Achaea, was abundant not only in merchants thronging to it, but also in highly learned men and the pursuit of the highest arts. Tarentum,[78] Rhegium,[79] Naples obviously were repositories not only of riches, but also of the Greek arts and disciplines. Capua and Antioch[80] became famous not as much 20 for their many citizens, the strength of their fleets, and their merchandise, as for those arts by which youth is shaped into humanity. We know from Strabo[81] and Tacitus[82] that Marseille too, the port of Gallia Narbonensis, once was a great city for the study of languages and arts. Indeed Rome, the goddess of 25 countries and nations, was able to busy itself with conquering the world and barbarism at the same time; to arrange an army while establishing the rules of speech; to give a dictator command of an army camp while listening to orators speaking in the Forum.

---

78 Now Taranto, a port in the heel of Italy.
79 Reggio di Calabria.
80 A great port in Antiquity, whose ruins lie near modern Antakya (Turkey).
81 Strabo, *Geography* 4.1.5.
82 Tacitus, *Annales* IV 44, *Agricola* 4.2.

rationes subducere videantur, qui ob diversarum nationum frequentationes, disciplinarum ornamenta et omnem elegantem doctrinam à civitatibus arceri cupiunt.

Quod si praesentia magis movent, Venetos spectate, in quorum
5   amplissima urbe, publicae facundiae non mercatorum tumultus, non Adriatici maris fluctus, non ipse Leonis (quem insignibus ostentant) rugitus obstrepit. Lutetia Parisiorum, hominum multitudine fervet, tumultuatur, sordet. Nec tamen alienum putavit Carolus Magnus, et post hunc multis seculis Francis-
10   cus I. ingeniorum gloria regalis solii majestatem irradiari: aut indecorum fore, si vendentium ementiumque litibus eruditae Sorbonensium lites permiscerentur. In Vbiis Colonia, in Pannoniis Vienna, in Boiohaemo Praga, in Vandalis Rostochium, ad Viadrum Francofurtum, ad Vistulam Gedanum, in Vasconibus Burdegala
15   famae celebritatem à negotiationibus pariter, et honestissimo Scholarum otio consecutae sunt.

Quod si ad antiquorum tempora recurrere libeat, Inter mercatores Solon fuit, gravis Atheniensium legislator, inter mercatores Thales fuit, idem è Sapientum numero; et Socrates, ille oraculo Apollinis
20   sapientissimus. Quin et Plato (teste Plutarcho in vita Solonis) inter divinas animi meditationes, olei Venditione in Aegypto quaestum fecit. quorum autoritate tutus mercator, parum aestimare habebit,

So I think that those who want the beauty of the humanities and all elegant learning to be kept away from the cities because of the crowd from various nations are setting up a very bad argument.

If you find examples from the present more persuasive, look at the Venetians, in whose great city public eloquence is not drowned out by the merchants' tumult, the waves of the Adriatic or the roar of the lion that is the city's symbol. Paris boils over, is in uproar and is filthy with its multitude of people, yet Charlemagne, and many centuries after him François I, thought it fitting that the majesty of the throne should be illuminated by the glory of great minds, and becoming that the learned disputes of the Sorbonne professors should mix with the quarrels of buyers and sellers. In the land of the Ubians,[83] Cologne, in Pannonia[84] Vienna, in Bohemia Prague, in the land of the Vandals[85] Rostock, on the Oder Frankfurt, on the Vistula Gdansk, in Gascony Bordeaux, all have equally acquired fame with commerce and the honourable quiet of the schools.

And if you would like to go back to Antiquity: among the merchants was Solon, the dignified legislator of the Athenians; among the merchants was Thales,[86] also one of the wise; and Socrates, wisest of all by Apollo's oracle. Why, even Plato (as Plutarch tells us in his *Life of Solon*) between his divine meditations made a profit by selling oil in Egypt.[87] Protected by their authority, the tradesman can safely disregard the harsh words

83 A Germanic tribe living near the Rhine in Antiquity. Cologne was originally called Oppidum Ubiorum, 'Town of the Ubians'.
84 A Roman province that included eastern Austria.
85 A Germanic people of Late Antiquity; according to modern scholarship, however, present-day Rostock (on the German coast) was never part of Vandal territory.
86 Natural philosopher and scientist (6th century BC). One of the 'seven wise men of Greece', like Solon and Bias.
87 Plutarch, *Life of Solon* II 4.

quae in negotiatores acrius scripsere Gregorius, Chrysostomus, Augustinus et Cassiodorus.

Quae cum ita sint, beatam hanc Amstelodamensium Rempub. puto, in qua jam mercatoribus philosophari, et philosophis mercari concessum. Postquam enim summis prudentissimisque rectoribus studium fuit, ornamenta omnia dignitatis et praesidia stabilitatis amplissimae urbi quaerere, pomoeria diducere, turres attollere, portus fodere, classibus disjunctissimas terras adire; adhaec Orienti primum, mox et Occidenti armis instare, et sub invictissimis Nassoviae gentis Principibus, unà cum sociis urbibus, potentissimum hostem patriis finibus propulsare: tandem ad has quoque curas devoluti sunt, ut veram stabilemque gloriam huic loco à litterarum perennitate, ab ingeniorum cultura, et sapientiae praemiis vindicarent. ut quae civitas orbis penè Vniversi est receptaculum, jam quoque eruditionis audiat; quae totius penè Europae commune est aerarium, prudentiae thesauros recludat: quae mercium omnigenarum est custos, disciplinarum ac ingenuaɪum etiam artium sit promptuarium. Habuit jampridem multa, quae mirati fuerunt advenae. at nunc quod laudent. Obstupuerunt Germani, Britanni, Scoti, Cimbri, aedificiorum splendorem, navium in longum exporrectas stationes, spatiosam, potentem urbem; omnibus rebus, quas vel natura suppeditat, vel elaboravit ars affluentem. at nunc eandem praeceptis institutisquc Philosophɪae et literarum stabilitam sentient ipsi. Et erunt inter eos, qui posterius hoc prioribus praeferent, cum illa fortunae deberi videantur, at hoc omne consilii sit: illa annorum ac longioris aevi spolium sint, hujus verò fructus istiusmodi, qui per omnium seculorum memoriam vigebunt, quos posteritas venerabitur, quos ipsa aeternitas semper intuebitur.

20   ad aedificiorum *1643*

that Gregory, Chrysostom, Augustine and Cassiodorus wrote against merchants.[88]

Seeing all that, I consider the Republic of Amsterdam fortunate, where merchants are now allowed to philosophize and philosophers to conduct trade. For after its most distinguished and prudent rulers had decided to seek all the ornaments of dignity and protections of stability for this great city, to expand its boundaries, to build high towers, to dig harbours, to sail to the remotest lands with its fleets; moreover, to face in war first the East, and shortly after the West as well, and under the invincible princes of Nassau, together with allied cities, to drive a most powerful enemy out of the fatherland – they finally came to these cares as well, to claim true and lasting glory for this place based on the permanence of literature, the culture of minds and the rewards of wisdom. So that the city that is known as the receptacle of practically the whole world is now also known as that of erudition; the city that is the shared treasury of practically all of Europe now opens the coffers of prudence; the city that guards merchandise of all kinds is now a storeroom of sciences and honest arts as well. It already had many things about which newcomers wondered; but now it has something for them to praise. The Germans, Britons, Scots and Jutes were amazed by the splendour of the buildings, the long landing stages for ships, the spacious and powerful city, abundant in everything that either nature supplies or skill has made – but now they will sense that that same city is strengthened by the precepts and instruction of philosophy and literature. There will be those among them who prefer the latter to the former, since the former depend on fortune, but the latter is a matter of counsel entirely; the former is the prey of the years and progressing age, while the latter will bear fruit of the kind that lives on in the memory of all the centuries, that posterity will revere, that eternity itself will gaze at forever.

88   Besides Erasmus, these are the only Christian authors Barlaeus mentions.

Quare, ut unde exorsa est, eò se convertat oratio mea, vos allo-
quar, Reip. hujus rectores Amplissimi. Date manum et praesidium
nascenti Scholae, quae vobis natales suos hodie consecrat. De-
fendite, imò producite, non tam eos, quos egregiis praemiis huc
5   evocastis, quàm optimas artes, sine quibus parum ornata, parum
instructa, respublica aut fuit unquam, aut erit. Martem vestra ope
armatum vidimus, sensit Hispanus, navibus, auro, terris, etiam
ubi terras esse non credidimus, exutus. Iam Minervam, illam
eruditionis, humanitatis, sapientiae Deam, intra portas vestras ac
10   moenia recipite, non ut bella gerat, sed ut de veterum eam bellis
disserentem audiatis: non ut regna urbesque evertat, sed quibus
consiliis surgant cadantque, doceat: non ut res Romanorum ac
Graecorum ipsa gerat, sed loquatur: non ut mercari cives vestros,
sed sapere doceat. ut quae loca adeunt, quibus ventis navigant,
15   quod coelum mutant, quos populos peregrè frequentant, quas
merces emunt, qua fide, quo candore res augeri debeant, propius
ab eâ discant. Regum, Imperatorum, Principum laudatissimorum
vestigiis insistitis. Bibliothecam, hoc est, tot eruditarum mentium
commenta et lucubrationes, tot Sapientiae, et veritatis doctores
20   civibus vestris donastis. Iam insuper illos, qui vestris auspiciis,
quod in iis libris solidum, erectum et frugiferum est, viva voce
in animos diffundent. Gratias ergo vobis Reipublicae hujus, Ecclesiae, civium et modestissimae Iuventutis nomine ago, qui, si
bona sua norint, ratum habebunt, quod dixi: si non norint, discent
25   propediem, quantum sit cum doctrinâ virtutem imbibisse.

24   norunt *1632*

Therefore, so that my speech may return to where it began, I will
address you, most honourable rulers of this republic. Give your
help and protection to the school that is born and that today
consecrates its beginnings to you. Defend, indeed advance, not
as much those whom you have invited here with great rewards   5
as the humanities, without which no republic ever was or ever
will be ornate and well provided. We have seen Mars armed with
your help; the Spaniard has felt it, robbed of his ships, gold, lands,
even where we did not believe there was land.[89] Now receive
Minerva, goddess of erudition, humanity and wisdom, within   10
the gates and walls of your city – not that she may wage war,
but that you may hear her discussing the wars of Antiquity; not
that she may overthrow kingdoms and cities, but that she may
teach by what counsels they rise and fall; not that she may act
like the Romans and Greeks herself, but that she may speak of   15
their deeds; not that she may teach your citizens to trade, but
to be wise; that no matter what places they visit, by what winds
they sail, where they move, which peoples they frequent abroad,
what goods they buy, they may learn more closely from her with
what faith and candour business should be increased. You are   20
following in the footsteps of the most famous kings, emperors
and princes. You have already given your citizens a library, that
is to say, so many speculations and nocturnal works of learned
minds, so many teachers of wisdom and truth. Now you have
moreover given them those who, under your auspices, by the   25
spoken word will instil into the minds all that is solid, upright and
fruitful in those books. So I thank you on behalf of this republic,
the church, the citizens and the modest youth – who, if they
know their riches, will confirm what I have said; and if they do
not, they will soon learn how important it is to have absorbed   30
virtue together with learning.

---

89   Likely a reference to the continuous competition in the New World between
the Dutch Republic and the Spanish monarchy. Perhaps Barlaeus more specifically
aims to recall the conquest of Brazil in 1630, following the capture of the Spanish
Treasure Fleet in the Bay of Matanzas in 1628 by Piet Hein.

Vos verò viri nobilissimi, spectatissimi, doctissimique, sive
cives, sive advenae estis, animis, linguis Illustri huic gymnasio
favete. Erit hic, ubi perfuncti negotiis, animum componetis,
ubi afflicti solatium petetis: ubi inopinato lucro aucti mentem
5   temperabitis ab insolenti laetitia: ubi audaciae in exponendis
mercibus occursabit prudens timor; timorem moderabitur fiducia,
fiduciam scientia, scientiam recti conscientia. Si patres estis,
volupe mihi erit de liberis vestris benè mereri: si non estis, de
vobis ipsis. Etenim in hoc nati sumus, in hoc educati, ad hoc
10   vocati, ut ea, quae didicimus, non nostra sint, sed et aliorum. Tum
demum vos profecisse scitote, cum litteras, et earum professores
aestimare didiceritis. Hactenus fines possessionum propagare
studuistis, in latifundiis totos lacus absorbuistis, trans Oceanum
villicos misistis. nullibi non fluminum ripas aedificia vestra,
15   villae, praedia praetexunt. Iam discite majorem et spatiosiorem
esse Sapientiam, quae divina omnia et humana, praeterita et
futura, coelum, terras, maria complectitur. Preciosarum rerum
pompam in domibus vestris explicatis. at pretiosior Sapientiae ac
literarum supellex, in qua auro, argento, gemmisque omnibus plus
20   fulgent virtutis et honesti praecepta, in qua hoc ad precium facit,
quod per fortunam non obvenit; quod sibi illam quisque debet,
nec pravis artibus paratur. Cum mercium, quae in hanc urbem
advehuntur, molem, varietatemque conspicitis, naturae exiles
particulae in conspectum veniunt. cum Philosophia occurret,
25   simillimum toti naturae spectaculum videbitis. Magnum vos
aliquid praestitisse putatis, cum Gallias, Germaniam, Hispa-
niam, Africam, Indiam annis aliquot obivistis, et quidem itinere
laboriosissimo, et tot periculis circumsepto. Philosophi animus
haec omnia coram videt, coram lustrat, omnia velocius, quam Sol
30   ipse, obit, et obit quoties vult, discriminum omnium securus. Sed

And you, most noble, respected and learned men, whether you are citizens or immigrants, be kind to this school in your minds and in your speech. This will be the place where, having finished your business, you will calm your minds, where you will seek comfort if you have suffered a loss; where after an unexpected gain you will moderate your minds from extravagant joy; where audacity in offering merchandise will be countered by prudent timidity; timidity will be regulated by confidence, confidence by knowledge, knowledge by conscience. If you are fathers, it will be my pleasure to do well by your children; if you are not, by you yourselves. For in this we were born, in this we were raised, to this we were called: that that which we have learnt is not ours, but belongs to others as well. Know that you will have made progress once you have learnt to value literature and its teachers. Thus far you have endeavoured to extend the limits of your possessions, in your lands you have drained entire lakes, you have sent overseers over the ocean; there is no place where your buildings, villas and manors do not fringe the river banks. Now learn that wisdom is greater and more spacious, embracing all things divine and human, past and future, the sky, the earth, and the seas. You display an arrangement of precious items in your homes, but more precious is the outfit of wisdom and literature, in which gold, silver and all jewels are outshone by the lessons of virtue and honour; in which the price is determined by that which does not come to one by fortune – because all owe wisdom to themselves, and it cannot be obtained by crooked tricks. When you survey the mass and variety of the goods brought into this city, you see little bits of nature. When philosophy presents itself, you will see a spectacle that is very similar to nature as a whole. You think that you have done something great when you went to Gaul, Germany, Spain, Africa and India in the course of some years, and by a very difficult route too, beset by so many dangers. The philosopher's mind sees all these things right before it, examines them up close, goes everywhere faster than the sun itself and goes there as often as it wishes, safe from all dangers. But I would like to ask you, wrenching a confession from you even

libet quaerere ex vobis, ut vel invitis confessionem extorqueam, Annon Philosophiam expeteretis, si beneficiaria, si lucrosa, si utilis esset? affirmabitis opinor. At qui beneficiaria non sit, quae rerum omnium uberem scientiam suppeditat? qui lucrosa non sit, quae menti lumen, voluntati sanctitatem, affectibus ordinem ac quietem largitur? Has opes cum possideat Sapiens, non minus opulentus est, quam vos, non minus splendidus, quam vos, non minus beatus, quàm vos. Et profectò si callidi rerum aestimatores, fundos, agros magno aestimant, quia his pignoribus minus noceri posse credunt, quanti putabitis aestimandam eruditionem, quae nec incendio eripitur, nec naufragio absorbetur, et inter ipsas regnorum concussiones ac motus inconcussa manet.

Vos denique Adolescentes et Iuvenes, quotquot adestis, parentum vestrorum solatium et amor, Reip. hujus spes, erudita propago, eum quoque ad hanc rem animum conferte, qui egregiis exercitationibus erudiri, et bonae mentis succo imbui cupiat. Tum magni eritis et sapientes, cum placere vobis coeperint Sapientiae prisci ac primi inventores, Plato et Aristoteles. quorum severa lectione non solum intellectum à foedo ignorantiae situ vindicabitis, verum etiam de hostibus vestris, ira, voluptate, libidine, audacia, ambitione, prodigalitate triumphabitis, idque eò gloriosius, quo plus est, sibi, quàm aliis imperasse. Ne vitam credite illam, quam ex aëre trahitis, sed quam ex studiis; nec splendidum putate auro vel argento circumfulgere, sed doctrinae luce. dum alii pecunias numerant et ad stateram expendunt, vos Sapientum verba et voces: dum alii aes, piper, linum, ponderant, vos philosophiae momenta. dum alii peregrinantur, fluctibus jactantur, aut latronum saevitiam experiuntur, vos domi intellectum per illustrium scriptorum monumenta securi circunferte, et dum Morinorum

against your will: Would you not aspire to philosophy if it were beneficial, profitable, useful? I think you will say yes. But how would it not be beneficial, as it supplies plentiful knowledge of all things? How would it not be profitable, as it gives radiance to the mind, holiness to the will, and order and quiet to the passions? As the wise man possesses these riches, he is no less affluent than you are, no less dazzling than you are, no less happy than you are. And indeed, if clever assessors set great store by estate and lands because they think that with these securities they are less susceptible to loss, how highly do you think one should value learning, which does not burn down in a fire, does not go down in a shipwreck, and remains unshaken even when kingdoms are shaken and in uproar?

And you, youngsters and young men who are here, your parents' solace and love, this republic's hope, cultured offspring: to this matter you should also bring a spirit that desires to be shaped by excellent exercises, to be imbued with the juice of reason. You will then be great and wise when you will have begun to like the ancient inventors of wisdom, Plato and Aristotle. By reading them with discipline you will not only liberate your intellect from the filthy mould of ignorance, but also triumph over your enemies: anger, pleasure, desire, audacity, ambition, prodigality, and all the more gloriously as it is more important to be one's own master than other people's. Do not believe that your life is what you draw from the air, but that it is what you draw from your studies; do not think it splendid to have the shine of gold or silver around you, but to shine with the light of learning. While others are counting their money and weighing it in a pair of scales, you should be weighing the words of wise men; while others are weighing bronze, pepper and flax, you should be weighing the importance of philosophy. While others go abroad, are tossed by the waves, or experience the brutality of robbers, you should let your minds wander around the works of famous authors in the safety of your homes, and while the audacious sons

spolia repetunt audaces Neptuni filii, vos doctorum hominum commentationes, quas posteritatis esse voluerunt, in usus vestros, Dei inprimis gloriam, Patriae ac Ecclesiae salutem convertite.

Dixi.

of Neptune reclaim the loot of the Dunkirkers,[90] you should turn the meditations of learned men that they wanted to share with posterity to your own use, and most of all to God's glory and the welfare of fatherland and church.

Thank you.   5

---

90   The Dunkirk privateers were employed by the Spanish crown.

Bibliography

Primary Sources

Barlaeus, Caspar, *Mercator sapiens, sive Oratio de conjungendis mercaturae & philosophiae studiis: habita in inaugurationem Illustris Amstelodamensium Scholae* (Amsterdam 1632).

Coornhert, Dirck Volkertsz., *De Coopman: Aenwysende d'oprechte conste om Christelyck ende met eenen gelycken moede in 't winnen ende verliesen coophandel te dryven* (Norden 1580).

Beschryvinge van Amsterdam, haar eerste oorspronk uyt den huyze der heeren van Aemstel en Aemstellant: met een verhaal van haar leven en dappere krijgsdaden (Amsterdam 1665).

Elslandt, Boëthius van, *Lyk-Reden op 't overlyden van den wydtberoemden Caspar van Baerle, Doctor in de Medecijnen en Professor van de gantsche Philosophie in de doorluchtige Schole tot Amsterdam, uitgesproken door Johannes Arnoldus Corvinus* (Amsterdam 1648) (Dutch translation of Joannes Arnoldus Corvinus' speech: *Oratio in obitum viri celeberrimi Casparis Barlaei, Medicinae Doctoris, et in illustri Schola Amstelodami universae Philosophiae Professoris: recitata in auditorio statim a funere 19. Ianuari 1648.*

Briefwisseling van Caspar Barlaeus (1584-1648), after the edition of Geeraerd Brandt (Amsterdam 1667), edited by Marjolein van Zuylen and. A.J.E. Harmsen, available online: www.let.leidenuniv.nl/Dutch/Latijn/BarlaeusEpistolae.html.

Secondary sources

Berkel, K. van, 'Rediscovering Clusius: How Dutch Commerce Contributed to the Emergence of Modern Science', in *BMGN – Low Countries Historical Review*, vol. 123, no. 2 (2008) 227-236.

Blok, F.F., 'Caspar Barlaeus, de filosoof van het Athenaeum Illustre' in C.L. Heesakkers, C.S.M. Rademaker and F.F. Blok, *Vossius*

en Barlaeus: Twee helden die der dingen diept en steilt'afpeilen.
Het Athenaeum Illustre en zijn eerste hoogleraren (Amsterdam
1982) 24-32.

Blok, F.F., *From the Correspondence of a Melancholic* (Assen 1976).

Bostoen, K., 'De Van Elstlands: Een Haarlems Poëtengeslacht' in
E.K. Grootes (ed.), *Haarlems Helicon: Literatuur en Toneel te
Haarlem vóór 1800* (Hilversum 1993).

Bostoen, K., 'Zo eerlijk als goud: de ethiek van de wereldstad'
in Herman Pleij (ed.), *Op belofte van profijt. Stadsliteratuur
en burgermoraal in de Nederlandse letterkunde van de middeleeuwen* (Amsterdam 1991) 333-346.

Cook, H., *Matters of Exchange: Commerce, Medicine and Science
in the Dutch Golden Age* (New Haven 2007).

Dudok van Heel, S.A.C., *Van Amsterdamse burgers tot Europese
aristocraten. Hun geschiedenis en hun portretten. De Heijnen-
maagschap 1400-1800* (The Hague 2008).

Elias, J.E., *De Vroedschap van Amsterdam 1578-1795* (Amsterdam
1963).

oPistolarium, available online: http://ckcc.huygens.knaw.nl/
epistolarium/.

Frijhoff, W., 'Het Amsterdamse Athenaeum in het academische
landschap van de zeventiende eeuw' in E.O.G. Haitsma Mulier,
C.L. Heesakkers, P.J. Knegtmans, A.J. Kox and T.J. Veen (eds.),
*Athenaeum Illustre. Elf studies over de Amsterdamse Door-
luchtige School 1632-1877* (Amsterdam 1997) 37-90.

Harmsen, A.J.E. and E. Hofland, *Caspar Barlaeus: Bibliografie
van Caspar Barlaeus of Kaspar van Baerle (1584-1648)*, available
online: www.let.leidenuniv.nl/Dutch/Latijn/BarlaeusBiblio-
grafie.html.

Heesakkers, C.L., 'Foundation and Early Development of the
Athenaeum Illustre at Amsterdam' in *Lias*, vol. 9, no. 1 (1982)
3-18.

Heesakkers, C.L., 'Het Athenaeum Illustre' in C.S.M. Rademaker
and F.F. Blok, *Vossius en Barlaeus: Twee helden die der dingen
diept en steilt'afpeilen. Het Athenaeum Illustre en zijn eerste
hoogleraren* (Amsterdam 1982) 1-10.

Hell, M., 'De oude geuzen en de opstand. Politiek en lokaal bestuur in tijd van oorlog en expansie 1578-1650' in W. Frijhoff and M. Prak (eds.), *Geschiedenis van Amsterdam. Centrum van de Wereld 1578-1650* (Amsterdam 2004).

Israel, J., *The Dutch Republic: Its Rise, Greatness and Fall, 1477-1806* (Oxford 1995).

Kamerbeek, W.G. 'Some Letters by Johannes Arnoldi Corvinus' in *Lias*, vol. 9, no. 1 (1982) 86-109.

Keblusek, M., 'Mercator Sapiens: Merchants as Cultural Entrepreneurs' in B. Noldus and M. Keblusek (eds.), *Double Agents: Cultural and Political Brokerage in Early Modern Europe* (Leiden and Boston 2009).

Lesger, C., *Handel in Amsterdam ten tijde van de Opstand. Kooplieden, commerciële expansie en verandering in de ruimtelijke economie van de Nederlanden ca. 1550-ca. 1630* (Hilversum 2001).

Lesger, C., 'Merchants in Charge: The Self-Perception of Amsterdam Merchants, ca. 1550-1700' in M.C. Jacob and C. Secretan (eds.), *The Self-Perception of Early Modern Capitalists* (New York 2008) 75-97.

Lis, C. and H. Soly, *Worthy Efforts: Attitudes to Work and Workers in Pre-Industrial Europe* (Leiden and Boston 2012).

Mak, G., 'De kooplieden van Amsterdam: Leve Spinoza, leve Gümüs, leve de mercator sapiens!' in *De Groene Amsterdammer* (30 November 2002).

Mak, G., 'Wij, de elites van nu, missen noblesse oblige' or 'Wij, de elite van deze tijd, zijn veel te bang' in *NRC Handelsblad* (18 April 2015).

Miert, D. van, *Humanism in an Age of Science. The Amsterdam Athenaeum in the Golden Age, 1632-1704* (Leiden and Boston 2009).

Molhuysen, P.C., *Bronnen tot de geschiedenis der Leidsche Universiteit*, 5 vols., (The Hague 1913-1924), vol 2.

Molhuysen, P.C., P.J. Blok et al. (eds.), *Nieuw Nederlandsch Biografisch Woordenboek*, 10 vols. (Leiden and Amsterdam 1911-1937), vol. 4.

Netten, D. van, *Koopman in Kennis: De uitgever Willem Jansz Blaeu in de geleerde wereld (1571-1638)* (Zutphen 2014).

Peters, M., *De wijze koopman: Het wereldwijde onderzoek van Nicolaes Witsen (1641-1717), burgemeester en VOC-bewindhebber van Amsterdam* (Amsterdam 2010).

Petit, L.D., *Bibliographische lijst der werken van de Leidsche hoogleeraren van de oprichting der hoogeschool tot op onze dagen*, vol. 1 (Leiden 1894).

Prak, M., *The Dutch Republic in the Seventeenth Century: The Golden Age* (Cambridge 2005).

Rademaker, C.S.M., 'De vrijdom ga sijn' gang' in C.L. Heesakkers, C.S.M. Rademaker and F.F. Blok, *Vossius en Barlaeus: Twee helden die der dingen diept en steilt' afpeilen. Het Athenaeum Illustre en zijn eerste hoogleraren* (Amsterdam 1982) 12-23.

Rademaker, C.S.M., *Life and Work of Gerard Vossius*, 1577-1649 (Assen 1981).

Rademaker, C.S.M., 'The Athenaeum Illustre in the Correspondence of Gerardus Johannes Vossius', *Lias*, vol. 9, no. 1 (1982) 19-55.

Rauschenbach, S., 'Elzevirian Republics, Wise Merchants, and New Perspectives on Spain and Portugal in the Seventeenth-century Dutch Republic', *De Zeventiende Eeuw*, vol. 29, no. 1 (2013) 81-100.

Secretan, C. (ed.), *Le 'Marchand philosophe' de Caspar Barlaeus. Un éloge du commerce dans la Hollande du Siècle d'Or. Étude, texte et traduction du Mercator Sapiens* (Paris 2002).

Spies, M., 'De Koopman van Rhodos. Over de schakelpunten van economie en cultuur', *De Zeventiende Eeuw*, vol. 6 (1990) 166-173.

Sutton, Elizabeth A. *Capitalism and Cartography in the Dutch Golden Age* (Chicago 2015).

Velema, W., and Arthur Weststeijn (eds.), *Ancient Models in the Early Modern Republican Imagination* (Leiden and Boston 2017).

Weststeijn, A., *Commercial Republicanism in the Dutch Golden Age: The Political Thought of Johan and Pieter de la Court* (Leiden and Boston 2012).

Worp, J.A., 'Caspar van Baerle I. Zijne jeugd, studententijd en predikambt (1584-1612)', *Oud-Holland*, vol. 3 (1885) 241-265.

Worp, J.A., 'Caspar van Baerle II: Barlaeus als onder-regent van het Statencollege (1612-1619)', *Oud-Holland*, vol. 4 (1886) 24-40.

Worp, J.A., 'Caspar van Baerle III. Zijn verder verblijf te Leiden (1619-1631)', *Oud-Holland*, vol. 4 (1886) 172-189.

Worp, J.A., 'Caspar van Baerle III. Zijn verder verblijf te Leiden (1619-1631). Vervolg', *Oud-Holland*, vol. 4 (1886), 241-261.

Worp, J.A., 'Caspar van Baerle IV. Eerste jaren te Amsterdam (1631-1635)', *Oud-Holland*, vol. 5 (1887) 93-126.

Worp, J.A., 'Caspar van Baerle V. Zijn verder verblijf te Amsterdam (1635-1644)', *Oud-Holland*, vol. 6 (1888) 87-102.

Woude, S. van der (ed.), *Mercator Sapiens. Oratie gehouden bij de inwijding van de illustere school te Amsterdam op 9 januari 1632.* Dutch translation and introduction by Sape van der Woude (Amsterdam 1967).

Index

For Product Safety Concerns and Information please contact our EU
representative GPSR@taylorandfrancis.com
Taylor & Francis Verlag GmbH, Kaufingerstraße 24, 80331 München, Germany

www.ingramcontent.com/pod-product-compliance
Lightning Source LLC
Chambersburg PA
CBHW060311100426
42812CB00003B/746